LiVING TOGETHER

Philip St. Romain & Lisa Bellecci-st.romain

LoVING TOGETHER

A SPIRITUAL GUIDE TO MARRIAGE

LIGUORI
PUBLICATIONS

One Liguori Drive
Liguori, MO 63057-9999
(314) 464-2500

ISBN 0-89243-788-X
Library of Congress Catalog Card Number: 94-73020

Cover design and illustration by Christine Kraus

Table of Contents

Introduction

This is my commandment:
love one another as I love you.

John 15:12

The primary vocation for all Christians is to love. In married life, we are invited to love another person so completely and intimately that our lives become one. No other kind of human relationship has the possibility of such a profound union. Paradoxically, a healthy, loving union also empowers each partner to develop his or her individual personality to the fullest. Marriage provides the ideal situation for living and growing in the deepest of all human loves.

This is the ideal and some experience its reality. Many, however, do not. Instead of being united in love, couples are enmeshed codependently. Instead of becoming more whole in marriage, they experience despair, loneliness, low self-esteem, and dashed hopes. Their commitment is eroded. When marriage goes well, there is perhaps no greater human happiness; when it goes poorly, there may be no greater misery!

In writing this book together, we want to assure our readers that we know both the joyful and painful sides of married life. We have been married over eighteen years and have learned many important lessons along the way. In our work of counseling, lay ministry, writing, and public speaking, we have been fortunate to meet many people who have taught and supported us in our relationship. From these experiences, we have come to base our marriage on three important convictions:

- God's love is always present, ready to bless our marital relationship.

- We both must be committed to making our marriage our most important human relationship.

- Loving one another in a healthy manner requires more than just an act of will. We need specific skills and knowledge if love is to flow freely.

When we married, we had an abundance of faith in and commitment to each other. Faith and commitment kept us together when pride, hurt feelings, misunderstandings, and miscommunication tempted us to throw in the towel. We lacked the knowledge and skills we needed to enable our love to flow freely. Once we learned to communicate effectively and accept each other's personality type, our love came alive and stayed alive!

In this book, we will share with you our experience and understanding of skills which enable love to thrive within a marriage. Without a personal commitment to each other,

LiVING
TOGETHER

these skills will have little value. But a couple with commitment and even a small amount of faith will discover that these skills will help them begin to feel love for each other again or deepen the love they already share.

How To Use This Book

Knowing about a skill and possessing it are two different things. To possess a skill, you must understand what it is, you must want to use it, and you must practice, practice, practice. When practicing, you will make many mistakes; don't get discouraged. Keep on practicing. Sooner than you imagine, the skill will become habitual.

To give you an opportunity to practice together, we provide opportunities for you to reflect separately and together on how you experience the various lessons discussed in each chapter. We also provide practical suggestions on how to use these skills in everyday life.

We invite you to make a commitment to read the first three chapters together and practice the suggested exercises before you decide whether this book will make a difference in your marriage. Complete the first three chapters within a week; if you decide to continue, try to do at least one chapter each week. Give yourself at least one hour per chapter and come together when you will not be disturbed by children or the phone.

If you decide to go through the book together, we encourage you to pray for each other in a special way. Let this be a time of growth and renewal for your marriage; ask God to bless your efforts. This is prayer according to God's will. God wants your marriage to be a living sign of love for all to see. This is what we mean when we say that marriage is a sacrament.

Part One: HEALTHY COMMUNICATION

Chapter One
Listening With Your Heart

*I will give you a new heart
and place a new spirit within you.*

Ezekiel 36:26

We begin this book with a section on communication because these skills play a pivotal role in fostering a healthy relationship. In married life, there are good times and bad. The hard times test a relationship. Couples who know how to listen to each other, to share feelings appropriately, and to renegotiate their expectations of each other not only survive the troubling times but grow closer together. Those who do not know how to communicate make things worse with their tongues; they become more hurt and distant from each other.

In Part One, we will emphasize four basic communication skills: listening, affirming, sharing feelings, and asserting. With these four skills, you can at least talk about any problem without making things worse. More positively, these skills can help you more fully enjoy conversing with each other. The fruit of healthy communication is intimacy. When a couple experiences intimacy, happiness is not far behind.

 ## PHIL

When I first began dating Lisa, I enjoyed listening to almost everything she talked about. I liked the tones of her voice and her expressiveness as she enthusiastically related the happenings of her day. In addition, I had read enough from Fr. John Powell's books on relationships to know the importance of listening. So I made it a point to give her my full attention when she had something important to tell me.

But after we married and began to experience the stresses that come with keeping a job, doing daily chores, adjusting to each other's needs, parenting, and keeping social obligations, listening became a struggle for me.

I was frequently too tired or preoccupied to give her my full attention. There were times when she tried to confront me about something I did that bothered her or asked me to do something I didn't particularly want to do. I frequently failed to listen to her and also became defensive, making matters worse. I listed her shortcomings or tried to justify my behavior with a variety of intellectual principles that really had nothing to do with the present issue. Consequently, Lisa felt ignored and discounted and our relationship was strained.

To become a better listener, I have had to learn to lower my defenses to hear what Lisa says before I respond. The most important listening skill I have learned is validation. When she shares something important with me, I still note my inner reaction, but I also make a conscious effort to let her know I hear what she is saying. If, for example, she shares a frustrating experience, I wait until she is finished and then reply, "Pretty frustrating!" This lets her know that I hear her feelings. I try to validate her opinions, too, when she shares them with me. Validation does not mean that I always agree with her; it only lets her know that I hear her. She needs this from me and I need it from her. Listening opens me to Lisa's world, which I am learning to enjoy and appreciate more and more each year. When I fail to listen, I am left with only my world. According to a saying I first heard in my native Louisiana, the most lonesome place in the world is "Bayou Self." I do not want to live there, especially not in marriage. And so I try to listen.

LISA

When I learned to drive a car, I learned to drive defensively. My instructor cautioned that though it may be my turn and I may be "in the right," if the other driver didn't stop, I would be "dead right." I finally realized that I was being "dead right" a lot in our marriage—and it was killing us. I was shocked when I realized this because when I wear my "social worker hat," I am a great listener and negotiator! Listening skills such as giving the other person my full attention, making nonverbal gestures and expressions to show I'm following the speaker's ideas, and listening for the unspoken feelings are skills that I use very naturally when I'm in a listening mode. And it seemed that I could be in such a mode with everyone except my husband—the one person who matters the most!

That's where being "dead right" came in. I wanted to win. Many times I *knew* I was right so I would push for my way or my plan. And though I often got what I wanted, I felt hollow inside. I now know that I felt this way because I had slashed our relationship when I insisted on getting my way. When I dealt with others, I didn't put issues in a win-lose perspective and could let the conversations flow and unfold. To get out of the win-lose attitude with Phil, I had to stop and quietly tell myself: "This marriage, this relationship with this man, is more important than winning." Sometimes, when my pride was so entrenched and my fear of an uncertain outcome was so strong, I felt I was dragging myself out of a boxing ring. Sometimes I thought I'd choke on the pride I had to swallow so I wouldn't verbally fight. Yet every time I have taken the risk of refusing to see an issue as win-lose and, instead, have listened and acknowledged his point of view, I've won.

We both have a commitment to consider the other person's point of view, and trusting in that helps me to give up insisting on my way. The rewards of trusting are the creative solutions we find and the bond of intimacy that grows each time we discuss an issue considerately, showing care for the other.

The Skill of Listening

To learn and grow in the skill of listening, practice the following:

1. Give the other your *attention*. There are times when it is not necessary to give full attention, but in any important conversation, nothing less will do. Notice what is being said as well as the nonverbal dimension of the message (tone of

voice and body language). Make it your goal to see and feel what your spouse says from his or her perspective. If you begin to react internally while your spouse is speaking, simply notice your reaction and keep paying attention. You'll have your turn to speak later.

2. *Validate* what you hear—especially the predominant emotion. Let your spouse know what you have heard by saying, "So you felt *(feeling word)*," or "Sounds like it was pretty *(feeling word)*." It is not necessary to do this after every sentence. Eventually you will develop your own style of timing and word choice.

3. *Clarify.* If you're not sure what kind of message you were supposed to get, ask. This is especially important when your spouse wants you to respond with a particular action.

Obstacles to Listening

People have difficulty listening for several reasons including:

- lack of practice
- fatigue
- preoccupation with something else
- no interest in what the other person is saying
- a defensive attitude, especially if confronted

Common Defenses

Defenses usually rise when we feel hurt and angry about what someone tells us. Defenses minimize the impact of the message. One harmful consequence is that we really can't hear another person when we are defensive. Some common defenses include:

analyzing	generalizing	projecting
attacking	glaring	protecting
blaming	grinning	rationalizing
complying	intellectualizing	shouting
debating	interrupting	silence
defying	joking	staring
denying	judging	switching topics
evading	justifying	threatening
explaining	minimizing	withdrawing
frowning	questioning	

Dialogue Exercise

Take a few minutes to reflect individually on the questions below. We recommend that each of you write your responses to each question, then come together to share your reflections with each other. Remember to pay attention, to validate, and to clarify when necessary.

1. On a scale from one (very poor) to ten (very good), how do I rate myself as a listener? How do I rate my spouse? What are my reasons for these ratings?

2. Which of the obstacles to listening apply to me? When do I experience these obstacles? What obstacles to I recognize in my spouse?

3. When I don't like what I hear and begin to feel hurt and angry, what defenses do I most commonly use? What defenses do I see my spouse using?

4. How do my defenses affect my spouse and our relationship? How does my spouse's defensiveness affect me?

5. What commitment am I willing to make to improve my listening? What change do I want my spouse to make?

Daily Practice

In three different conversations each day, make a more conscious effort to:

- pay attention to the verbal and non-verbal messages of another person (it doesn't have to be your spouse)
- validate the predominant feelings, opinions, and expectations
- ask for clarification when the message is not clear

Practice will help these listening skills become a habit.

Chapter Two
Affirming the Good

Refuse no one the good on which [they have] a claim / when it is in your power to do it.

Proverbs 3:27

You may think there isn't much to learn about affirmation as a skill. Doesn't it simply mean to say nice things to people?

That's part of it, but we must be careful to avoid indulging a counterfeit form of affirmation called approval. Affirmation is very good for relationships; approval is very bad.

To distinguish between affirmation and approval, consider two aspects of our experience: our personhood and our behavior (in philosophical terms, being and doing). We affirm the personhood, or being, of someone through smiles, hugs, the words "I love you," and other words and gestures. Being-level affirmation says, "I like you because you're you."

No behavior is mentioned. It is best to affirm the personhood of others when they haven't done anything particular to merit affirmation. They know then that you love them because they exist and not for any other reason. This kind of affirmation is a form of unconditional love.

You can affirm the behavior of others by telling them how you feel about what they did. You must be specific about the behavior: "I like the way you cleaned the living room. It looks inviting."

A smile of gratitude goes well with such a remark but don't verbally affirm personhood at that time. That's what approval does—links personhood and behavior. "I love you because of what you do" is the message of approval. This is conditional love, the destroyer of all relationships. Conditional love implies, "If you love me because of what I do, then how will you feel about me when I do something wrong? You will disapprove of me, right?" The subtle difference is an important difference. Affirmation builds relationships; approval and disapproval destroy relationships.

 ## LISA

I learned to affirm my husband through our children. I saw them as vulnerable, their self-concepts developing; they needed affirmation. Why should my grown, adult husband need it too? He was competent in his job, helpful at home, diligent with yardwork. He was doing what he was supposed to do; what was there to say? I vividly remember the occasion that changed my perspective. After complimenting our two preschool girls on the good job they had done, I was surprised when Phil asked, "What about me? Didn't I do a good job too?" I thought he was joking and maybe he was, in a way. His question made me think: Why not? I complimented the children easily. Why was it so hard for me to compliment adults, especially my husband? Was it because I felt competitive with adults? Was I too busy noticing a few minor corrections that needed to be done that I failed to see the major portion of a task already done well? Was I concerned that adults would think I was complimenting them because I wanted something from them? Was I stuck in the habit of taking for granted those things others were "supposed" to do, things that "required" no gratitude?

While I considered my motives, I reflected on how I felt when I received compliments. The more specifically a compliment related to a task I had done and the more the compliment focused on how my task helped someone, the more genuinely pleased I felt. But when I received the generic "We appreciate you!" given to everyone else at the school where I worked, I found it hardly registered within me. I also began to notice how I felt when I gave compliments. (This was hard for me to do at first if the adult's job was less than perfect or incomplete!) I began to sense that I wasn't in this alone, that there was an inter-relatedness of individuals needing one another, each contributing to the whole. I gradually let go of my perfectionism, giving the good work someone had done the credit it deserved. As I became more secure, I became less stingy with genuine compliments, at home, at work, and at church.

Though I have grown in recognizing and affirming others and their work, I have not forgotten the children who first started me on this path. Our weekly family meetings begin with compliments. But affirming the children and Phil must go beyond words. My actions affirm them, too, when I sit and listen to Phil after each work day, when I stop and share a hug "for no reason," and when I allow adaptations to "my" ideas! And I experience Phil's affirmation of me; he is more accepting of my pace and my many projects. As usual, the unexpected outcome of affirmation, whether compliments or actions, is the feeling of unity and intimacy.

PHIL

Like many others, I was raised in a culture where affirmation was uncommon. As long as I did what I was supposed to do, no one said much. When I "messed up," however, I was confronted. To receive positive comments, I had to either look very good or do something better than others. This conditioning still influences my behavior and attitudes. I find it hard to believe that ordinary, everyday things in my life are worth affirming.

This attitude about myself extended to others, including Lisa. As long she did what she was supposed to do (what I expected her to do), I said little. When she looked very good or did something special, I affirmed her; when she failed to live up to my expectations, I almost always let her know. To make matters worse, I felt treated the same way. After several years, we both felt unappreciated even though we knew we loved and cared for each other. We allowed lots of hurt feelings to accumulate through insufficient affirmation.

During the past few years, I have worked hard to change this attitude and behavior. I try to be less critical and to give positive comments to Lisa whenever possible. I may say something as simple as telling her she looks pretty or that I noticed she has done some housework. I also try to tell her every day that I love her. At first, I felt awkward and "mushy" saying these things. My old conditioning got in the way and I was afraid she would find me weak, corny, and unmanly. Her warm, appreciative smiles reassure me that she enjoys being affirmed. When I look for goodness and beauty in Lisa, I find more of these qualities in her, and thus my feelings of attraction for her continue to grow.

I have also discovered that I, too, need affirmation more than I realized. Though I know she loves me, I like to hear Lisa say it. Intellectually, I know we will always be here for each other. But her affirmation helps me feel loved and special. It might not be manly according to my old understanding of "a man," but I enjoy feeling loved, special, and appreciated. I am more of a man when this vulnerable side of my nature is awake! Living with this vulnerability is possible because of Lisa's loving affirmation. Without it I would be reluctant to drop my old conditioning.

Dialogue Exercise

1. Make a list of five things your spouse does that you appreciate. Be very specific about times recently when you have been grateful for this behavior. (Focus on the behavior. Do not talk about the person.)

2. Do you feel loved and affirmed as a person by your spouse? What does your spouse do to communicate this being-affirmation?

3. What are three qualities of character you admire in your spouse? (For example, honesty, gentleness, discipline.) Describe times when you have observed these qualities in your spouse.

Daily Practice

The following suggestions will help you develop the skill of affirmation.

- Be attentive to making eye contact and smiling at your spouse.
- Take the initiative in hugging and making other affectionate contact with your spouse. Say "I love you" through physical touch as frequently as possible.
- Tell your spouse "I love you" at least once each day.
- If your spouse does something you admire and appreciate, share this.
- If you hear something nice about your spouse from someone else, pass it on.

Chapter Three
Feelings and Intimacy

The community of believers
was of one heart and mind.

Acts of the Apostles 4:32

People express emotions in a variety of ways. Four common methods are:

- Repressing: The emotion is held inside or "stuffed" so that no one—perhaps not even you—knows what is going on.

- Acting Out: You do whatever the emotion moves you to do. If sad, you cry; if fearful, you run away; if you find something humorous, you laugh; if angry, you raise your voice and become aggressive.

- "You" messages: You do not speak directly about your feelings but about the behavior and circumstances which affect you and the motives you assume others have. This is one way to blame others and circumstances for your feelings: "If you cared about me, you would come home on time."

- "I" messages: You speak directly about how you feel and about the behavior and circumstances that affect you: "When you come home late, I feel angry and worried."

Emotions are neither morally right nor wrong. *How* we express our emotions, however, *is* a moral issue. Are we hurting someone? Are we truthful? Are we growing closer together or drifting apart?

Are there instances when repressing or acting out emotions is preferable to calmly stating them? Yes, but these should be exceptions to the usual way you communicate and you must take special care with anger. Repressed anger frequently becomes depression and anger acted out can become abusive.

Is the "you" message always wrong? Yes, even when you use it to express pleasant feelings. It is wrong because it makes others responsible for your feelings and assigns motives that others may not have. When combined with "acting out," "you" messages cause verbal and emotional abuse.

When you need to let others know how you feel, an "I" message works best. It allows you to speak directly about how you feel without judging or insulting. An "I" message allows your tone of voice and your body language to express your emotions. The danger of abuse is lessened because you do not judge motives, insult, or threaten.

LiVING
TOGETHER

An "I" message contains two parts: how I feel and what the feeling is about. For many people the hardest part is the first part—finding feeling words that identify the emotions being experienced. This takes practice but you will discover that the results are worth the effort.

PHIL

I have struggled with this kind of communication. It's not because I don't experience emotions. I do! But even when I'm feeling intense emotions, I tend to use logic to "get at the bottom of things" or to "set the record straight." There are times and places for logic, but it seldom fosters intimacy.

I finally learned that my "intellectualizing" and "moralizing" were ways I dealt with my emotional issues. These approaches, however, did not help Lisa. Sometimes my analysis became a judgment of her motives. Generally I seemed insensitive to her feelings and I needed to learn another way to deal with my emotions. I found help in the courses I took as I prepared to become an addictions counselor.

My tendency is still to "think things through" when either of us has an emotional issue to discuss. But now I know to check myself and speak directly about how I'm feeling. I've learned, for example, that it's better to say, "I feel disappointed that you didn't do the chore I asked" than to say, "Why don't you ever do the things I ask? Don't my requests mean anything?" In the second example, I'm judging motives—I'm assuming Lisa doesn't care. The first example contains no judgement, only a statement of how I feel about a neglected chore. This "I" message allows me to share my emotion without making Lisa feel defensive.

When we use "I" messages to share feelings and then really listen to each other, emotional intimacy deepens. This does not end the discussion, especially if we have a problem to solve. But knowing we can grow closer to each other even when dealing with problems gives me great consolation. To achieve this closeness, I know I must exercise great care about how I speak when I have uncomfortable emotions.

LISA

Have you ever had a heated discussion end abruptly with "Because I just don't want to, that's why!" I've been on the giving and receiving ends of such outbursts and I'm uncertain which feels worse. Yet I know that to get over the breach and on to sharing and intimacy, I must be honest about my feelings, especially with myself. My facial expressions let everyone else know how I feel even when I'm unaware that something has been triggered inside me. To acknowledge my feelings honestly, I must be quiet for a while, write in my journal, and talk out my feelings with myself without worrying that someone will say, "You shouldn't feel that way" or "Get over it; that's the way it is." If I can honestly face even my most unpleasant feelings, then I *can* start to "get over it." I can continue the discussion (with less "heat" now!) and let the other person know what's causing my fear, worry, or disappointment. For instance, when I'm overwhelmed by many project deadlines, it is really an intimacy-killer when Phil sarcastically says, "Oh, yes, you can do it all!" But if he simply validates my feeling, "Worried, huh?" then I can look at my problem without fighting him. As Phil has become more accepting of my feelings, my trust in him has grown; I now get to the "why" of those feelings more quickly. If he were to argue or be sarcastic with me, I know I would be tempted to blame him for the problem instead of going to my own heart.

Dialogue Exercise

Take this opportunity to practice the "I" message method of expressing emotions by sharing with each other your responses to the statements below. Remember to listen and to validate. If your discussion strays from the topics and one of you begins to use "you" messages, point this out. Try again to express the emotion with an "I" message.

1. I feel grateful when you

   _____.

2. When I think of our future together, I feel
   (feeling word) _____
   because_____.

3. Lately, I've felt anxiety about

   _____ because

   _____.

   (explanation may not be necessary).

4. An emotion I have trouble sharing with
   you is _____.
   I usually feel (the emotion) when

   _____.

5. I feel close and connected with you when

   _____.

LiVING
TOGETHER

Daily Practice

Spend at least 15 minutes together sharing your day. Usually people just talk about what happened. Share, instead, how you *felt* about what happened. Make a special effort to use the "I" message method when possible. This exercise can be combined with the Listening Practices suggested in Chapter One.

Chapter Four
Asking for Your Wants and Needs

In its own time every need is supplied.
Sirach 39:16

Ideally, couples approach a committed relationship to give and receive satisfaction of needs. But when one has a need and the other has the means to satisfy that need, an imbalance of power can result, leading to complications, manipulation, even abuse. We believe it is important, therefore, to label three patterns of interaction so that you can identify your and your spouse's needs. You can then make the changes necessary to more effectively communicate your needs and wants.

We will consider the passive, aggressive, and assertive patterns of interaction. Frequently females take a passive stance in the beginning of a relationship because society has defined *polite* and *loving* as "not making waves." This is a descriptor, not a rigid stereotype. Passive males and females experience much frustration because they often fail to get what they want. They express their frustration aggressively with outbursts of blame frequently followed by guilt; few people want to treat the ones they love so harshly. After the outburst the pendulum swings back to the passiveness of "whatever you want."

The solution to the pendulum is not to threaten "…or else," not to blame with "If only you had…," not to keep score with "You always…" and "You never…," not to use sarcasm like "It's about time!" These are aggressive stances that put the other person on the defensive. A variation on aggressiveness is passive-aggressive: saying "Yes," letting the other believe you, and then not following through. People who are angry but who do not feel powerful enough to say "No," outright will agree to something but not follow through. When this happens repeatedly in a relationship, it destroys trust.

Assertiveness is actually quite simple. It means asking directly and respectfully for some specific behavior. Two examples of assertive requests are:

- "Would you be willing to (name the specific behavior)?"

- "Please (name the specific behavior)."

Notice the absence of an explanation and a rambling introduction. Both examples are statements about a specific behavior. When one partner feels distant from the other, the assertive behavior could be to ask for some time to talk or go out together. Complaining "You don't love me anymore" or asking your spouse to "be close" is ineffective. But the request for time to talk is specific enough for a yes or no answer and has a definite beginning and end.

LiVING
TOGETHER

If assertiveness is so simple, why don't people use it?

- Some people are so angry about times they were passive or taken advantage of that they still seek revenge, even if it is on someone else.

- Others feel selfish when they *ask* for what they want or need. They prefer that the other person *offer* to do something without having been asked.

- Some fear that when they ask directly for something they will be refused. They are afraid of "no," associating it with rejection. If an imbalance of power exists in a relationship, the weaker spouse might be worried about using up all of his or her "favors." Instead, the passive person indirectly hints and the other is "selfish" when the hint is not taken.

- Many people have never learned how to communicate assertively. They do not know how to ask respectfully and they are not specific with their requests.

What about confrontation? Confrontation is a form of assertiveness. The communication formula resembles the assertive statements:

- "Would you please do/stop doing (specific behavior)?"

- "Please do/stop doing (specific behavior)."

As with the assertive skill, it is important to be very specific about the behavior that you want to see more or less of. If you feel angry or frustrated, begin with an "I" message that expresses your feeling. Sharing feelings and listening is insufficient, however. Sometimes you need something done differently; assertiveness and confrontation, therefore, have a place in a relationship.

If your initial request is not honored, then effective confrontation requires you to do something to take care of yourself or to impose logical consequences. Telling someone you will not continue a phone conversation unless the other person stops cursing you is a logical consequence and also a way to take care of yourself. Usually people will respond to confrontation when your request is reasonable.

 ## LISA

I remember the many times I have swung back and forth between passive "Do whatever you want" and aggressive "Why don't you ever ask what I want?" Phil surely must have been confused about what pleased me! I was confused too. I grew up knowing how to be polite, but politeness often was ineffective in my marriage. I was silent about my wants and needs, expecting Phil to cue in when I became quiet, slammed things, or talked sharply. I remained angry for several years, taking out on Phil my feelings about other issues. Fortunately, through courses and reading, I learned assertiveness skills. Gradually, with practice, I developed security in the knowledge that I could have my needs met without being aggressive. Somewhere I read about relationship rights: I have the right to ask for whatever I want. I also have the right to refuse any request. These rights have given me a great sense of freedom to both ask and refuse; I do not need to be a victim of anyone's unreasonable expectations. I have become more understanding when Phil chooses to refuse one of my requests. When something is really important to me, I negotiate or calmly find another way to get what I want or need. Our home environment is more honest and satisfying since we've implemented these skills.

These skills are effective with any need, large and small; even lovemaking wants and needs can be addressed assertively. If there is anything in your life together that you want changed—something grating on your nerves, something that would make life easier and more pleasant—tell your spouse.

 ## PHIL

When we first married, I expected Lisa to prepare coffee and breakfast for me every morning. Although we had discussed many details of married living before our wedding, we had neglected this. She didn't know I expected her to fix my breakfast, although I thought she did. Therefore, no breakfast awaited me each morning. At first I felt hurt, then I became angry. *What was the matter with her?* I wondered, *Was she lazy? Forgetful?* After a few weeks, no longer able to make excuses, I confronted her about it. I learned she had never agreed to cook my breakfast and didn't plan to begin. I had brought this expectation to our marriage from my own growing-up experience; my mother always fixed breakfast for our family and I naturally thought my wife would do the same. Lisa, however, wanted to use her time in the morning for other activities; because I was capable of fixing my own breakfast, I agreed. Later, when Lisa did prepare breakfast for me, I was grateful; when she didn't, I felt neither hurt nor anger. Changing my expectations eliminated one area of disharmony in our relationship.

Through the years, I have discovered other expectations I brought to our marriage. Many were based on the roles I saw my parents acting out during my childhood. Each time I encountered an unfulfilled expectation I experienced the familiar hurt and anger. In each instance we had to acknowledge our feelings and struggle together to find solutions.

One of the greatest obstacles to asking for my wants and needs was my belief that Lisa should know them without my asking or telling her. When I reversed the perspective, however, I realized I could not read her mind. I also realized that often I agreed to perform tasks only to forget them. I discovered Lisa also sometimes forgot; undone chores were oversights rather than deliberate snubs. I now know I have a responsibility to ask for my wants and needs even when I have asked for them many times before. When she remembers without my asking, it is a nice bonus.

Another difficulty for me has been confrontation. How could I ask her to stop doing something without being too harsh or indirect? The communication method we have described has helped me. When I use these skills, Lisa and others usually respond positively. Making direct and respectful requests is more effective and beneficial than trying to control Lisa or hinting at my needs.

Dialogue Exercise

1. Which of the obstacles to assertiveness do you have? Which do you recognize in your spouse?

2. Make a list of things you would like your spouse to do more of to help you grow closer in your relationship and in your home life. Be specific.

3. Make a list of specific behaviors you would like your spouse to do less of to help you grow closer in your relationship and in your home life.

4. When you share your lists from exercises #2 and #3, you may receive positive responses to some requests and negative responses to others. Celebrate the positive agreements with a hug. The negative responses can be dealt with through negotiation, the topic of the next chapter.

Daily Practice

Whenever you want your spouse (or anyone else) to do more or less of a certain behavior, use the assertiveness method described in this chapter.

When you think your spouse or someone else is using an indirect method to ask you for something, clarify the request using the assertiveness formula. When your spouse complains about a messy room, respond, "So you're upset about the messy room (validation), and you're asking me to pick up the newspaper when I'm through reading it (assertiveness)." Make every effort to avoid the indirect methods of communication.

Chapter Five
Reaching Agreement

Do two walk together / unless they have agreed?

Amos 3:3

The goal of negotiating is to reach agreement together on a particular issue. The process usually goes through four stages:

1. One person makes an assertive request but the other does not agree to the request.

2. Both partners state why they want what they want. This step can include sharing feelings and values as well as specific issues.

3. Both partners validate the other's request and the rationale for the request.

4. Both partners explore outcomes acceptable to each, seeking solutions that allow both partners to get

most of what each wants. The partners use one of the following strategies:

- Synthesize: to put things together so both can get what each desires: "You want to go into town to shop and I want to eat out. Why don't we go into town to shop *and* eat out?"

- Compromise: to take turns granting each other's requests or to give up a little of what each wants so the couple can still do something together.

These four stages can be pursued step by step, but it is often possible to go from Step 1 to Step 4 without spending much time explaining and validating. This is especially true when negotiating small decisions pertaining to daily routine. When decisions involve significant commitments of time and money, we recommend working through all four steps.

Sometimes agreements cannot be reached after working through the negotiating process. If there is no rush, then agree to disagree for now; try negotiating later after both of you have had time to think and reflect. You may still find agreement impossible. In such instances, you may need to pursue your interests separately or seek counseling.

Obstacles to Negotiation

There are many reasons why the negotiating process breaks down. Three of the most common are

LiVING
TOGETHER

- rigid attachment to traditional roles

- selfish unwillingness to compromise, even when this entails no violation of your ethical principles

- passive submission to the request of the other, even when this entails a violation of your ethical principles

These obstacles make it difficult for couples to reach healthy agreements on even simple requests. Assertive requests become win-lose situations rather than opportunities to grow closer together in love. Because these obstacles frequently cause hurt feelings, anger, and resentment, couples need to see them as barriers to love and work to eliminate them. The four steps of negotiation provide couples with an excellent discipline for growing together in love.

 ## PHIL

When I was a child, I learned there were certain responsibilities that belonged to women and others that were appropriate for men. My parents, grandparents, uncles, aunts, neighbors—practically all the adults I knew—seemed to live according to these gender-defined roles. The men earned the money; the women stayed home and raised the children. The men did yardwork and maintained the automobiles; the women cooked the meals and cleaned the house. Everyone seemed to know what each was expected to do.

Naturally, my concepts of male and female roles were influenced by what I heard and observed as I grew. I even recall hearing teachings in church that supported these traditional roles. I reached adulthood with a strong set of convictions about what men and women "should" do. Lisa had had a similar upbringing and seemed to share my convictions about many aspects of these roles. When we first married, we both assumed we would assume the roles we had seen modeled for us by earlier generations.

Soon, however, we faced situations where traditional gender-defined roles were inadequate. When our first daughter was born, Lisa was in graduate school and worked part-time. Academic and child-care responsibilities left little time for cooking and cleaning house. Moreover, I enjoyed cooking more than Lisa and she liked some kinds of yardwork more than I.

At first it was hard for me to let go of the traditional roles, but eventually I realized we needed to decide for ourselves how we wanted to do things based on our own strengths and weaknesses and the tasks that needed doing. We had to learn to negotiate and I found this difficult. I had never been taught how to negotiate and, more important, I feared that if I let go of the traditional roles I would not know what it meant to be a man.

This fear has been resolved. Roles do not define man or woman. Through negotiation we share our wants and our feelings. Negotiation deepens our sense of freedom and responsibility. I believe now that life is always changing and that couples who learn to negotiate are more likely to grow together than couples who try to "force" life to conform to roles that don't work for them.

LISA

During my childhood I got my start in the art of negotiating. Each Halloween my sisters and I came home with the bags of candy we'd collected, dumped them in our own piles, and prepared to trade. We subdivided the candy into smaller piles: the "No Way" pile, our favorites that we'd never trade; the "Definitely" pile, candies we didn't like; and the "Maybe" pile, the goodies we would consider trading, depending on the offer.

Negotiations in marriage are obviously more important than my early candy trades yet there are some similarities. On some issues I won't budge—maybe in a few months or years but definitely not now. With other issues, once I hear Phil's reasoning or his feelings, I'm willing to compromise. Two elements help us move through the process: not all issues are equally important to both of us, and each of us has a different degree of competence and interest in particular areas (a new car purchase, schools for the children, vacation destinations, home decorating). When we reach an impasse, I must remember that I'm not in a life-or-death situation! I don't have to feel threatened! We can talk, listen, and maybe temporarily postpone a decision. My goal is not to "win" but to continue a loving relationship with my husband.

Dialogue Exercise

1. On a scale of 1 (poor) to 10 (great), how well do you think you and your spouse negotiate? Give reasons and examples to support your judgement. Share this with your spouse.

2. With which obstacles to negotiation do you identify? Which do you experience when you try to negotiate with your spouse?

3. If you did not receive a positive response to your assertive request in the Chapter Four dialogue exercise, use this request now as Step One and begin the negotiation process. When you share your request this time, invite your spouse to offer a counter-request. Go through the four negotiation steps; try to reach the stage of synthesis or compromise.

4. If you did receive a positive response in Chapter Four, or if you want to negotiate on another issue, choose a topic to discuss with your spouse. Begin by formulating the issue in an assertive request; be sure to get in touch with your feelings and values underlying the request. If your spouse does not agree to your request, work through the four steps of negotiation. Remember to validate each others' feelings.

Daily Practice

Continue to notice when you and your spouse experience obstacles to negotiation. When your spouse experiences one of the obstacles, point this out gently and respectfully. When you notice obstacles within yourself, share this with your spouse.

Part Two:
UNDERSTANDING OUR PERSONALITIES

Chapter Six
Starting Off—The Two Attitudes

I praise you, so wonderfully
you made me.

Psalm 139:14

Because human nature is enormously complex, any attempt to classify human personalities will necessarily be inadequate. The approach we use in Part Two is the system developed by Dr. Carl Jung. Many people are familiar with Jung's psychological types through the Myers-Briggs test. The popular book, *Please Understand Me: Character and Temperament Types* by David Keirsey and Marilyn Bates, also uses Jung's psychology. We have found his system one of the most helpful tools for understanding ourselves. The system doesn't explain everything about who we are, but it gives us one way to identify some basic personality tendencies.

In this section, we will introduce the most basic concepts of Jung's psychological types. We will proceed step by step, providing explanations and checklists to help you and your spouse recognize your similarities and differences.

If you already have an understanding of your personality, or if you prefer to wait to do this section later, feel free to skip ahead. Each of the four main sections is self-contained.

Jung's method for determining personality types examines opposing tendencies in our human consciousness. The first pair of opposites we discuss is extroversion and introversion. Jung first described these "two attitudes" and brought them into our everyday vocabulary.

The two attitudes—extroversion and introversion—are concerned with the basic flow of our energy and attention. The extrovert finds the "outside world" of people, places, things, and circumstances most interesting. Naturally, then, the extrovert focuses on adapting to this outer world. The introvert is more interested in the "inner world" of ideas, images, symbols, and impressions. Strongly developed introverts are sometimes oblivious and uninterested in the outside world, except when external events and movements affect the inner world. Introverts focus on adapting to the inner world.

Neither an introverted nor an extroverted disposition is better than the other; surveys indicate the population is evenly divided between these two natural tendencies. Later we will discover that all persons possess both tendencies. For now, you need to determine your dominant tendency.

Use this simple checklist from *Tracking the Elusive Human*, an excellent book on Jung's psychological types written by our friends Jim and Tyra Arraj. For each question, evaluate both your introversion and extroversion on a scale of 1 to 5, with 5 indicating the strongest agreement. After taking the test, tally your points in each column. Next, go through the checklist again, this time rating your spouse.

	Introversion	Extroversion
When speaking to strangers, I...	sometimes hesitate ___Self ___Spouse	find it quite easy ___Self ___Spouse
When I am in a new group, I tend to...	listen ___Self ___Spouse	talk ___Self ___Spouse
People describe me as...	quiet and reserved ___Self ___Spouse	open and easy to know ___Self ___Spouse
When learning a new subject I like to...	read about it ___Self ___Spouse	hear about it ___Self ___Spouse
With money I tend to...	save ___Self ___Spouse	spend ___Self ___Spouse
When planning a dinner, I prefer having...	four people ___Self ___Spouse	twelve people ___Self ___Spouse

LISA

My parents comment that once I learned to talk, the whole world knew what was going on in our family! When I was twelve, I was in an elevator with my grandfather and began talking to a stranger when my grandfather immediately ordered me to be quiet. I was quite startled; I was just making conversation!

Phil and I are in different places on the introversion/extroversion scale. I love being where the action is (or might be!) and come home revitalized. He prefers quiet walks, time alone, small and less frequent gatherings. Before we knew about the two "attitudes," we had difficulty understanding each other. At social gatherings, even after church, I wanted to stay and talk with everyone, but Phil was always ready to go home early. Each of us was frustrated. When I had an issue to discuss, Phil wasn't ready to talk about it immediately but wanted time to think. I thought he was stubborn or that he refused to take me seriously. The introversion/extroversion theory has helped us understand and accept each other.

Couples who are opposites in introversion/extroversion need to make adjustments. The extrovert needs to sacrifice some outside involvements to have time to develop a deeper relationship with the introverted spouse. The introvert needs patience when the extrovert talks about everything to everyone everywhere, realizing that the "talker" still loves and is interested in the introverted partner. As you learn more about your personality types, you will be amazed how you can complement each other and help each other grow!

PHIL

When I was young, my parents and others said I was shy. I disliked large gatherings, even with family members. I preferred playing alone, finding it difficult to make new friends. The few friends I did have were very close. During high school I didn't ask a girl for a date because I was unsure about what to say or do if one agreed to go out with me. Though these are all characteristics of introverts, I was unaware of them then. I thought I was shy and unsociable and often felt guilty about not being more outgoing or interested in other people.

Since then I have developed my extroverted side a bit more. I am definitely an introvert but am more comfortable now about meeting strangers and engaging in "small talk." I am also more willing to share what's going on in my life if I believe someone is genuinely interested. Living with Lisa has helped me develop my extroverted side. Because she is interested in others and willing to talk to them about almost anything, I frequently find myself becoming interested also.

There are still times, however, when I'd rather leave the crowds behind and just go home. Waiting for Lisa while she talks to others is then difficult, but I know that's how she is. When I refrain from joining her, she knows I'm being me. Accepting our introversion and extroversion has helped us become more comfortable with ourselves and with each other.

Dialogue Exercise

1. Give examples of introverted and extroverted behavior in yourself and in your spouse.

2. How do introversion and extroversion contribute to harmony and struggles in your relationship?

3. How can you show increased respect for and support of your spouse's basic attitude?

4. How do you want your spouse to show increased respect for and support of your basic attitude?

Remember to listen and validate as you take turns sharing.

LiVING
TOGETHER

Chapter Seven
What's Next?—
The Four Functions

*There are different kinds of spiritual
gifts but the same Spirit.*
1 Corinthians 12:4

In *Man and His Symbols*, Jung eventually concluded that "extroversion and introversion are just two among many peculiarities of human behavior. If one studies extroverted individuals, for instance, one soon discovers that they differ in many ways from each other, and that being extroverted is therefore a superficial and too general criterion to be really characteristic." Perhaps you had the same thought as you considered the extroverts and introverts you know. Therefore we must continue our study of personality types by looking at the "four functions" of our consciousness which are divided into the categories of perceiving and judging. Perceiving considers what comes into our consciousness; judging deals with the decision-making process.

The Perceiving Functions

The two opposing ways of perceiving are sensing and intuiting. Like introversion and extroversion, sensing and intuiting are not like two sides of a coin but rather like two ends of a continuum with extreme sensation at one end and extreme intuition at the other. Most of us find ourselves between the two extremes, using both sensation and intuition in our everyday lives. You will probably discover, however, that you use one function more than the other.

Sensate types pay more attention to information that comes through the five senses: Can I see it? hear it? taste it? touch it? feel it? Sensate personalities notice the details of the environment around them and they live in the present. At work and at play they enjoy having a plan and meticulously execute details of the plan.

Intuitives, on the other hand, notice very few details of their environment. They need only a bit of factual information to stimulate their minds to immediately "see" the possibilities in a situation. Their imagination constantly works with alternatives; options are "real" to them. Intuitive perceivers live in the future, sometimes becoming impatient with and neglectful of details and planning.

These are a few general characteristics. Use the checklist below from *Tracking the Elusive Human* to determine your preferences. Rate your intuitive and sensate responses to the questions below using a scale from 1 to 5, with 5 indicating the strongest agreement. After rating yourself, use the checklist to rate your spouse.

LiVING
TOGETHER

	Intuition	Sensation
I tend to...	get excited about the future. ___Self ___Spouse	savor the present moment. ___Self ___Spouse
When I have set plans...	I feel tied down. ___Self ___Spouse	I am comfortable with them. ___Self ___Spouse
If I were to work for a manufacturer, I would prefer...	research and design. ___Self ___Spouse	production and distribution. ___Self ___Spouse
I tend to...	get involved in many projects at once. ___Self ___Spouse	do one thing at a time. ___Self ___Spouse
If people were to complain about me, they would say...	I have my head in the clouds. ___Self ___Spouse	I am in a rut. ___Self ___Spouse
People describe me as...	imaginative. ___Self ___Spouse	realistic. ___Self ___Spouse
When I find myself in new situations, I am more interested in...	what could happen. ___Self ___Spouse	what is happening. ___Self ___Spouse

Total your points in each column. Which is stronger?

The Judging Functions

The two judging functions—thinking and feeling—refer to how we make judgments and decisions using information that comes into our awareness through sensation and intuition.

Jung used the word *thinking* to refer to a preference for logical analysis. Everyone thinks about things, but thinkers in the Jungian sense are people who approach problems and circumstances systematically. You might describe them as "cool" and "tough-minded" as they proceed, step by step, to the source of something. Truth and justice take precedence with thinkers, even if their decisions upset others.

Feeling, according to Jung, is different from *emotion*. Everyone—even the thinker—has emotions. Rather, feeling is that part of our reason that is sensitive to the emotional and social consequences of decisions. Where the thinker is concerned with what is "right," the feeler is concerned with how everyone will be affected by a particular decision. Feelers want everyone to be happy; for them, it is often worth bending the rules to make that happen.

These fundamental differences between thinking and feeling can cause frustration in relationships. Generally, most men are thinkers and most women are feelers and therefore most marriages are a pairing of opposites. When important decisions must be made, most women want to do what makes others happy and most men want to do what is logical. When a couple is unaware of this, they can feel misunderstood and invalidated during their discussions. The thinker considers the other's reasoning illogical and the feeler finds the other insensitive. Hurt feelings and defensive walls result when you forget that both thinking and feeling are valid and complementary ways to reach a decision. Couples who understand this can accept their differences as a gift rather than a curse.

As with extroversion-introversion and intuition-sensation, thinking and feeling are two opposing potentials on a continuum. Most feelers are capable of logical analysis and most thinkers are aware of the need for harmony. Nevertheless, most people prefer to use one of these functions more than the other. Use the checklist below from *Tracking the Elusive Human* to determine your preference by rating the thinking and feeling responses below on a scale of 1 to 5, with 5 indicating the strongest agreement.

	Thinking	Feeling
People consider me...	reasonable. ___Self ___Spouse	warm, sympathetic. ___Self ___Spouse
When people argue, I want them to...	suggest a solution. ___Self ___Spouse	stop. ___Self ___Spouse
When someone has a problem, my first reaction is to...	help them solve the problem. ___Self ___Spouse	sympathize. ___Self ___Spouse
When I make decisions, I tend to use...	my head. ___Self ___Spouse	my heart. ___Self ___Spouse

LISA AND PHIL

Just a brief note here. We are both on the intuitive side of the scale but our attitudes are different. For example, Phil's intuition relates to the ideas in his mind (introverted intuition) while Lisa has these never-ending ideas about interacting with others or pursuing one of her many projects (extroverted intuition). We're typical of the male/female split on thinking and feeling when making decisions. Phil's frustrated, "You're just not thinking!" means the logic of the situation isn't being considered. Thinking is occurring, however. The thoughts are about what will bring harmony.

We can complement each other with these opposites. When Lisa needs to make a tough decision or follow-through an unpopular course of action, Phil's logical analysis is helpful. Simply making the comment, "You'll need to be left-brained on that one," is supportive. When Phil is in a decision-making conflict, he will lead with the logical analysis. After a time, there comes an appreciation for the feeling side of the situation. What we've learned is to give each other a little space and time to round out our approach.

Dialogue Exercise

1. Spend some time comparing your evaluations of self and spouse from the two checklists in this chapter. What events and habits influenced you as you rated yourself and your spouse?

2. How do intuition and sensation bring harmony, tension, or both to your relationship? Give specific examples.

3. How do thinking and feeling bring harmony, tension, or both to your relationship? Give specific examples.

4. What do you need your spouse to do more or less of to accept you and your perceiving and judging preferences?

Daily Practice

During the day be more attentive to the four functions discussed in this chapter. Notice which functions you use and when you use them. Notice too which functions your spouse uses—and when.

Chapter Eight
And Now—The Eight Basic Types

*As one face differs from another, / so
does one human heart from another.*

Proverbs 27:19

Now we are ready to take the insights of Chapters Six and Seven and put them together, recognizing that introversion and extroversion are attitudes expressed through the four functions. For example, thinking can be extroverted or introverted. The same is true with intuiting, sensing, and feeling. This combination of the two attitudes and the four functions gives us the eight basic types:

—Introverted Sensing (IS)
—Extroverted Sensing (ES)
—Introverted Intuition (IN)
—Extroverted Intuition (EN)
—Introverted Feeling (IF)
—Extroverted Feeling (EF)
—Introverted Thinking (IT)
—Extroverted Thinking (ET)

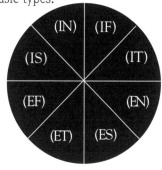

LoVING
TOGETHER

To determine your primary type, use your scores and what you learned in the previous two chapters as you respond to the following questions:

1. Are you more attuned to facts and details (sensation) or to possibilities (intuition)? Is this attuning focused within you (introversion) or on the world outside you (extroversion)?

   - Choose from the four possibilities below to determine your perceptual preference.

     IS   ES   IN   EN

   - Read the descriptions in Appendix One to confirm your choice.

2. When you make decisions and judgments, are you more likely to consider logical principles (thinking) or how you and others will feel about your decision (feeling)? Is your decision formed by inner consideration (introversion) or by external criteria or how it will affect the outside world (extroversion)?

   - Choose from the four possibilities below to determine your judging preference.

     IT   ET   IF   EF

   - Read the descriptions in Appendix One to confirm your choice.

3. To determine which of the two choices above is your "primary function," decide which is the strongest and most comfortable or natural for you. Your second choice is your "auxiliary function" that works closely with the primary. You can double-check your choice of primary function by noting its opposite on the pie graph; it will be your least developed or "shadow" function.

LISA

Learning about our personalities this way was like turning on a light bulb for me. With a primary EN type, I'm both blessed and doomed to be involved in many projects, rarely completing any of them and leaving lots of clutter that usually doesn't disturb me! My shadow side is the IS, which means I'm pretty weak in dealing consistently with daily details. I know that to finish something completely, I have to "will power it" through because I've lost enthusiasm for the project. It has ceased to be fun or creative. This remains a weak point for me. I've found, however, that my "shadow" side works well when I relax: I enjoy gardening, sewing, playing the piano, and even making charts.

PHIL

My primary function is IN. While Lisa's creative projects are going on in the outside world, mine are focused within. My intuition "sees" the connections between ideas and principles and my thinking function (the auxiliary) tries to bring some order to them.

Sorting these within myself sometimes requires periods of silence and solitude. Writing is also helpful.

My least-developed function is ES. Like Lisa, I use this shadow side to recreate. Sitting outside, gardening, bird watching, and playing golf help me keep balanced. I can also use my IN tendency for rest, feeling energized and ready to use the primary and auxiliary functions again.

Frequently, Lisa's EN and my ES clash. My ES perceives her unfinished projects lying around the house as disorder. This clutter doesn't disturb her but it does bother me. I find relaxation almost impossible when surrounded by all this busyness. I ask her to pick up her things and she does, but it inevitably reappears. Before I knew about personality types I thought Lisa was inconsiderate, and I felt hurt and angry. Now I know it's as natural for her to have many projects in various stages of completion as it is for the sun to rise. I have stopped interpreting the clutter as a personal affront, but when it bothers me, I ask her to put away her things. She graciously complies but I know they will reappear again soon. And this pattern will probably continue through the years.

Dialogue Exercise

1. How do you experience your primary function in everyday life? Give examples.

2. How do you see your spouse using her or his primary function? Give examples.

3. How does your auxiliary function work with your primary function?

4. How do your spouse's and your primary and auxiliary functions complement each other?

5. What struggles have you and your spouse experienced because of your different primary and auxiliary functions?

Chapter Nine
Loving Our Differences

*Love and truth will meet; / justice
and peace will kiss.*

Psalm 85:11

Are you wondering if you are too different from each
other to make your marriage work? Don't panic. Differences
are there and the concept of the eight basic types can help
you make sense of those differences. Jung also theorized
that we are attracted to someone who is our opposite because we sense that the other "completes" us—we feel
"whole" when we are with our partner. The wonderful bonus in marrying your opposite is that your spouse can lead
you to and teach you about your neglected, weaker "shadow"
side if you are willing to learn.

This learning does not happen overnight, though; our
personalities have been developing for years. Jung noted that
most people show a preference for their primary function by
the age of seven. The auxiliary function (your second choice
in the Chapter Eight exercises) develops during early ado-

lescence. During young adulthood the third function (the opposite of your auxiliary) develops. The "shadow" or "inferior" fourth function (the opposite of your primary) demands attention around and after the age of thirty-five.

Take a moment to complete this chart with your complete type profiles. This "picture" can help you both better understand some of your differences.

	Wife	Husband
Primary Function	_____	_____
Auxiliary Function	_____	_____
Third Function	_____	_____
Shadow/Fourth/Inferior	_____	_____

Are you a marriage of complete opposites? You are if your primary functions are opposite; your inferior functions are opposites too. Relationships between complete opposites can have episodes of strong attraction but also intense misunderstanding. You see things or make decisions differently; only when each of you develops your third and fourth functions will you better understand each other. Keep in mind

LiVING
TOGETHER

that in a feeling/thinking opposite pair, the one who can list all the logical reasons is tempted to declare himself or herself the "winner" of an argument. Remember also that the one who desires harmony (the feeling type) seeks it in specific instances and for your relationship in general. For the good of your relationship you "logically" should avoid win/lose situations! Use the communication skills of validating and negotiating instead.

Marriages between partial opposites also present difficulties if you focus on the differences instead of your common strength. For example, EN and IN might have difficulty working through introversion/extroversion needs, but using your common intuition can help you brainstorm ideas that meet the needs of both partners.

What about partners who have the same typology? You will probably experience fewer misunderstandings than partially opposite couples, but you may neglect some parts of your life. For instance, if you are both intuitives you will never run out of ideas. But because you are also weakest in the sensate area you may easily overlook the details of maintaining your household and your relationship.

Why is it good to know about your weakest tendencies? Using your third or fourth function to relax when you get too much of your primary is restful and also helps you strengthen those weaker parts. For instance, extroverts can curl up with a book while introverts can teach a weekly class or give a talk. The more you develop all your functions, the more you can accept, understand, and enjoy your spouse. This requires a commitment to personal growth. People too attached to their primary and auxiliary functions will not experience this growth, will fruitlessly struggle in their relationships, and can experience severe mid-life crises. Attachment is common but overcoming it results in more energy, balance, and enjoyment in everyday life.

LISA

We've already mentioned our common weak sensate side. Having children really gave us opportunities to strengthen this side! When they were little, I was always dashing to the store or dropping by someone's house. Now I realize my extroversion was trying to reassert itself in the midst of all the child-care details! Those were the days when I needed to talk to some adult. When Phil was the first adult through the door, I unloaded on him. He, however, just wanted to be by himself after being surrounded by people all day. We agreed he would stop by the parish chapel after work so that when he did get home, he could be available to us. As time passed, I had more experience being quiet and alone. What I find now is that I'm less restless with the introverted side of me. I enjoy silence; I've come to depend on my quiet time each morning. During a day with too many disappointments, I regroup not by talking and complaining but by spending time alone with my journal and the Bible. Often, I find renewed energy from the insights gained in the quiet.

PHIL

One of the most helpful things I've learned in our study of Jung's psychological types concerns his idea of individuation. This refers to the process of becoming a whole person, and it includes learning to use the third and fourth functions.

When I work primarily out of my primary and auxiliary functions, I am utilizing my strengths, but I am also neglecting the other half of my personality. Because Lisa embodies that other half with her preference for feeling, I tend to cling to her to fill that gap within me. She could do the same, relying on my thinking—her third function. This kind of attachment could lead to an unhealthy dependency between us.

The solution is for both of us to make an effort to develop our third and fourth functions. My other half is really within me, not "out there" in the person of Lisa. By embracing my other side, I become more whole within myself. This means I must work to develop my third and fourth functions, feeling and sensation. Lisa, a feeler, can help me to learn about how feeling works, but she cannot be my feeling self. The more whole I become, the more I am able to love Lisa without dependently clinging to her.

LoVING
TOGETHER

Dialogue Exercise

1. Are you a marriage of opposites or partial opposites? If so, how does this contribute to a clinging to each other?

2. How do you recreate with your inferior function? What could you do to use this function more often?

3. How and when do you see your spouse using her or his third function? Give examples.

4. How and when do you see your spouse using her or his inferior function? Give examples.

Part Three: CHRISTIAN MARRIAGE IS A SACRAMENT

Chapter Ten
Marriage as Sacrament

*God is love, and those who abide in love abide in
God, and God abides in them.*

1 John 4:16

Remember when you were a child and during religion class you had to name the seven sacraments? At the end of the list was matrimony. No one you knew ever used that word so you probably had to ask an adult what it meant. You learned that it referred to Christian marriage, and like the other sacraments it was a sign instituted by Christ to communicate grace.

Many couples believe that matrimony is a sacrament they received at the wedding ceremony. They compare it to their concept of baptism and confirmation: you receive it once from a priest or bishop and thereafter live in a new order of grace because of the sacrament. This, however, is incorrect. First, the couple ministers the sacrament to each other. They marry each other; the minister or priest is a witness, receives their consent to marry in the name of the Church, and blesses their commitment. Second, the sacrament of matrimony is not received just once. The couple receives the sacrament from each other throughout their lives. Matrimony is living a sacrament with each other.

Many Catholics have been taught to reverence the real presence of Christ in the sacrament of holy Eucharist. But remember that the Church teaches that Christ is present to us in all the sacraments. How does this apply to matrimony?

We look again at Eucharist. The sacramental signs for Eucharist are bread and wine. During Mass these become the Body and Blood of Jesus Christ.

What is the sign of the sacrament of matrimony?

It is the love of husband and wife for each other. When a husband and wife love each other, they manifest the presence of God. In their love for each other, husband and wife are blessed by the real presence of God. When a wife and husband love each other, they are signs of Christ's loving fidelity to the Church (see Ephesians 5:32). Through this love for each other they reveal Christ's love for his Church.

Married couples are also instruments of the Holy Spirit because, through their love for each other, they communicate God's own love to each other. This love is the Holy Spirit. Through their struggles to live in this love, a couple is sanctified, made holy, by the Spirit. The word *holiness* in this context shares the same root as the word *wholeness*. Husband and wife are instruments used by the Holy Spirit to help each other become more whole and holy.

In their love for each other, wife and husband are empowered to love others also. Their love overflows, first to their children and then to the wider circle of family, friends, coworkers, and the world. A sacramental couple is generally active in their service to the Christian community. They discover together the blessing of ministry: love grows if you give it away. Thus a couple is moved to spread the grace of Christ.

To acknowledge that the grace of the sacrament of matrimony spreads the grace of Christ throughout the Church is to acknowledge that this sacrament is first to be a blessing for family life. "In our own time, in a world often alien and even hostile to faith, believing families are of primary importance as centers of living, radiant faith. For this reason the Second Vatican Council, using an ancient expression, calls the family the *Ecclesia domestica,*" or domestic church (*Lumen Gentium* 11, cited *Catechism of the Catholic Church*, 1656). The rippling effect of love beyond the family is the most common way this grace is spread throughout the Church.

Because a couple will never fully exhaust the grace of Christ given in the sacrament of matrimony, they live this sacrament until death. Even through periods of sickness and trial, the grace of Christ makes it possible for them to love each other and thus be a sign to the Church and an instrument of the Holy Spirit (*Catechism of the Catholic Church*, 774).

Christian marriage is the way most men and women make their journeys of faith toward union with God. We do not get to heaven by ourselves. As we make this spiritual journey with our spouse, we are given the sacrament of matrimony to help each other become the person Christ is calling each of us to be.

In this section, we will continue to reflect on different aspects of this sacrament. We hope these reflections will help you grow in faith and awareness of God's presence in your marriage.

PHIL

Knowing that marriage is a sacrament has been both a challenge and a blessing. It is a challenge because it makes me feel responsible for the kind of relationship we model before our children and the world. Is the love of God signified in our relationship? Can other people say about Lisa and me what the pagans said about the early Christians, see how they love one another? I want us to be this kind of sign and I want it to be genuine—not just a role we play to impress others.

Unfortunately we are far from perfect in our love for each other. Our weakness and sinfulness sometimes distort the sign we reveal. I regret these times but feel powerless to turn things around through my own will power and intelligence.

That's where the blessing of matrimony makes a difference. Lisa and I are not in this relationship alone. Christ is with us through all the twists and turns of married life. Because he wants us to signify his love for the Church, we can be sure that he will give us the grace to love each other. I ask him for the grace often and my prayer is answered in many ways—especially through forgiveness and through maintaining a sense of wonder and gratitude about sharing my life with Lisa.

LISA

I recall several situations that illustrate the essence of the sacrament of marriage. The first comes from the fifth grade religion classes I taught. During the discussion of marriage I always asked, "A priest marries the couple: True or False?" "True!" they'd shout. When I shook my head sideways they were surprised. "A deacon!" someone would volunteer, enjoying looks of admiration from the rest of the class. I'd still shake my head and they were stumped. Then we'd talk about the concept of the couple marrying each other and how active and purposeful that is. The priest acts as the Church's official witness but does not marry the couple.

Another illustration comes from the day, almost two years after our wedding, when I walked with a friend, sobbing and complaining to her about Phil and our struggling relationship. She was stunned that we were having trouble. She thought we had a "perfect" marriage because we were both very involved in church work. We both had the misconception that for marriage to be a sign of Christ's love for the Church, it must be struggle-free. Not so. Faithfulness despite the struggle—remember Christ hung in with his less-than-perfect disciples!—is the sign of love.

The final illustration comes from a discussion with a young woman who had doubts about her young man being the "right" one for her. One of the questions I suggested she consider was whether he brought out the best in her; did he encourage and support her quiet prayer time, her continuing education, her family and career plans? Those were the ways I felt Phil supported me once I let him know what I needed. Those were the things that helped me edge closer to wholeness and holiness.

Dialogue Exercise

1. Marriage is a sacrament. What does this mean to you?

2. How is your marriage a sign of God's love? Give specific examples.

3. What can you do to be more conscious of the sacramental nature of your marriage?

4. Has married life helped you to become a more whole person? Why? Why not?

5. Has your spouse become a more whole person since you married? Why? Why not?

Chapter Eleven
"I Take Thee..."

A lasting covenant I will make with them.

Isaiah 61:8

What makes a marriage a marriage?

"The Church holds the exchange of consent between the spouses to be the indispensable element that 'makes the marriage.' If consent is lacking there is no marriage" (*Codex Iuris Canonici,* cited *Catechism of the Catholic Church*, 1626). This consent is affirmed by the couple in front of the Christian community and witnessed by a priest or deacon.

A marriage, then, is a formal agreement between a man and a woman to give themselves to each other as husband and wife. This agreement has sometimes been called a contract because, in this century, the contractual concept conveys the idea of mutual obligations and privileges.

The Christian understanding of marriage goes beyond a contractual mentality, however. The Bible refers to the marriage union as a covenant. A covenant resembles a contract in its definition of the responsibilities of the two parties, but it also binds the people together in a personal relationship. Yahweh tells Israel, "You shall be my people, / and I will be your God" (Jeremiah 30:22). Similarly, the Church belongs to Christ and Christ belongs to the Church. Two parties in a covenantal agreement become family to each other. They no longer belong to themselves alone; they now belong to each other. "So [also] husbands should love their wives as their own bodies. He who loves his wife loves himself"(Ephesians 5:28). Wives also are to love their husbands as they love themselves.

PHIL

Consenting to be Lisa's husband is something I must do every day, sometimes several times each day. The alternative to this consent in my heart is living in the relationship because of a sense of obligation and duty. When that happens, being a husband and father becomes a role that makes me feel trapped. Even the good things I do from a sense of duty are worth very little to Lisa and me for they do not carry the energies of love. Moving beyond mere duty and obligation comes when I freely choose in my heart to be in relationship with Lisa and the children. I might still feel myself resisting the demands of the relationship but I choose to do it anyway. The transforming power of love takes root in these free choices and gives me peace of mind.

Continuous consent has become easier for me through the years because I have come to trust Lisa's commitment to our relationship. Sometimes one or both of us seemed to let work or the children become a greater priority than our marriage. We felt distant and estranged from each other during those times; our marriage was weakened. When we became aware of this, however, we were both willing to reaffirm the priority of married love over everything except loving God. The grace of married life returned.

Our experience confirms for me the quote from the Catechism cited earlier. Without the consent of both partners, a marriage cannot exist. I cannot be in covenant with Lisa by myself. I can offer myself to her as husband, but if she does not offer herself to me as wife, no marriage exists. Both parties must commit themselves to the other, and I try not to take for granted Lisa's constant willingness to be my wife. Her consent is beyond my control; I can do nothing to make her freely choose to love me. Sometimes this seems like a miracle, too good to be true, that Lisa continues to choose to be married to me! When I feel such wonder and gratitude I find it even easier to offer myself to her as husband.

LISA

Recently I've noticed examples of continuous relational consent: a baseball star chooses to skip the glory and money of the All-Star Game to spend time with family; an actress confirms, after completing a popular movie, that she will make only one per year so she can spend time with her family; a local baseball coach, when asked to coach two youth teams next year, jokes, "I'd have to sleep in your garage if I did that!" These people are aware of a family's foundation: our spouses and children need time with us. Sometimes it is difficult to give that time at home because of the temptation of popularity, power, and the need to please others. Yet, as our pastor shared during a homily, "I've been at many bedsides of the dying, and no one has yet told me they regret not putting in more hours at the office."

It took three years of full-time work in a school before I became aware of the pattern of closeness and distance in our marriage. We felt close to each other during July, but in August my attention shifted to school preparation. Evenings and weekends from September to May were also full of school preparations and meetings. In June, I collapsed. During the school year we didn't have time to talk, putter in the yard together, or go places as a couple. I rationalized by reminding myself how thorough I was, how I was ministering to all those students, how I was using all my gifts. But our marriage was on "hold." When I changed to part-time work, I made the mistake of increasing my volunteer time. I was as preoccupied as when I worked full time. Temptations had come in forms of opportunities for creativity, being with other people, using a variety of my skills and gifts, and the lure of admiration. Like those creeping garden vines that grow and curl despite continual pruning, the temptations kept encircling me. Eventually, enough good and intimate experiences with Phil made the temptations lose their power. But to get to that point, I had to remind myself that though my outside activities were worthwhile, the best thing for me was to curtail them so I could spend time with my husband. I experienced giving up those activities as a sacrifice but one I knew in my head and heart I needed to make for the sake of our marriage. The rewards have been worth the sacrifice.

Dialogue Exercise

1. If you were not yet married to your spouse, would you choose him or her as your spouse today? Why? Why not?

2. How do you choose to be husband or wife to your spouse?

3. What makes it difficult for you to freely choose to remain in this relationship?

4. How do you feel when you have neglected your spouse because of other priorities? How do you feel when your spouse has neglected you because of other priorities?

5. What can you and your spouse do to help your marriage be the priority in your lives that you want it to be?

Chapter Twelve
Sexual Lovemaking

The two of them become one body.

Genesis 2:24

Every sacrament has a ritual that celebrates the presence of God. For holy Eucharist, the ritual is the Mass. In married life, the "consent that binds the spouses to each other finds its fulfillment in the two 'becoming one flesh'" (Genesis 2:24, cited in *Catechism of the Catholic Church*, 1627). Sexual lovemaking is the ritual celebration of the sacrament of matrimony.

As with the other sacraments, however, a couple must have the proper frame of mind to benefit from the grace of the ritual. A couple who spend most of their time arguing or preoccupied will have a different experience of sex than a couple who give themselves to each other in acts of love and service whenever possible. Sex for the latter couple is enjoyment at all levels of our human nature; physical pleasure alone characterizes the lovemaking of unhealthy couples.

If sex is to be a sacramental experience, the couple must attempt to love each other as Christ loves the Church. Only then will they realize that their lovemaking is not merely an enjoyment of each other but also a blessing of Christ's own love. This blessing is given to strengthen the bond between husband and wife and, when the time is right, to bring children into the world.

The Church's teachings on sexual morality are intended to promote the sacramental nature of sex. Catholic couples are obligated to learn these teachings and to make every effort to obey them. The Church also teaches that we are obliged to act according to the dictates of our conscience (*The Catholic Catechism*, 1782). Only then can the free consent of a husband and wife to each other in sexual lovemaking be preserved.

 ## PHIL AND LISA

We decided to write the sharing section of this chapter together and to focus our sharing around the values we have found most important for preserving the sacramental dimension of sex.

We believe the issue of *intimacy* is extremely important. If we have not been loving to each other in our communication and negotiations, we will have little to celebrate when we come to make love. Our understanding of each other's personality has led to acceptance instead of gossip and complaints, and this contributes to the feeling of intimacy. Maintaining an attitude of loving consent and praying for the grace to love each other opens us to a deeper intimacy.

Frequency and *timing* are also significant factors. It is common for one spouse to desire sex more frequently than the other. Eventually the spouse with less desire will feel used by the partner with more desire and can develop negative attitudes toward sex. We have suffered with each other through this, and our best solution has been to set a schedule that provides an opportunity for both of us to renew our desire to come together again. The schedule enables us to anticipate and prepare ourselves for lovemaking. It also safeguards against the need to be constantly available to each other or wondering if the other will be receptive. The discipline of a schedule is not always easy to maintain because it sometimes frustrates spontaneity. We prefer a schedule rather than risk "sexual burnout," however.

Taking a few moments for *prayer* when we come together helps us to recall that our love for each other is really a sharing in God's love. We ask God to bless our lovemaking, and we believe that God delights in this request. A feeling of peace and closeness almost always accompanies our prayer time.

Of course, the *content* of the ritual is extremely important. Unlike other sacramental rituals, this one is private and designed by the couple themselves. How we give ourselves to each other is an opportunity for creativity and mutual enjoyment. We've found that if we remain open to changing the ritual, we discover new ways to give ourselves to each other in sexual lovemaking. What we've enjoyed has changed through the years. Rather than depend on "how to" manuals, we have given attention to what our needs are and responded to acceptable requests.

Therefore, we must *communicate* with each other about what we want and don't want. Asserting and negotiating skills might seem out of place here, but they are as relevant to the ritual of lovemaking as they are to any other aspect of married life. It is inappropriate for one of us to insist that the other do something he or she considers objectionable or undesirable. This would negate the essence of the ritual, the free consent to fully give ourselves to each other in love.

When our lovemaking is rooted in these values we feel renewed and our love is deepened. Small hurts are healed, stresses of daily living are relieved, and we feel whole and happy.

We also feel closer to God. Our giving of self to each other also helps us give ourselves more fully to God. The dynamic of surrender is the same in both marriage and in faith. Both are about entrusting one's life into the hands of another. Sacramental lovemaking deepens faith, and faith in turn opens a couple to the graces of sacramental lovemaking.

Finally, we believe that lovemaking enriches our family life. We have brought three children into this world as fruit of this relationship, and we are happy and blessed to have them in our lives. In some mysterious way our love for each other creates a spiritual environment in which they participate too. This spirit of love gives them security and trust in the goodness of life. Our sexual relationship has been *procreative* in both a biological and spiritual sense.

Dialogue Exercise

1. On a scale from one (very poor) to ten (very good), how do you rate your sexual relationship with your spouse? Explain your reasons for this rating.

2. How do you feel about how you and your spouse make decisions about lovemaking? What do you want to do differently?

3. How do you feel about the content of your lovemaking ritual? What do you like most? What do you want to do differently?

4. Does your lovemaking help your relationship grow? Explain.

5. How does your lovemaking help your faith grow? Explain.

Chapter Thirteen
Bonders: I, Thou, and We

*A three-ply cord is
not easily broken.*
Ecclesiastes 4:12

A relationship is a bond between two people or between a person and some other thing. When people say, "Our relationship is strong at this time," or "Our relationship is unraveling," they are referring to the bond that exists between them and the other person. This bond is the sense of "we" that develops when two people share their lives. Bonders, then, refer to the different ways that two people share their lives.

There are many kinds of bonders. Living together, raising children, hobbies, faith, prayer, values, communication, lovemaking, extended family, and work are the most common bonders. Some may be highly developed, others superficial. The degree to which a couple is connected by these and other bonders determines the strength of their relationship.

We have found the two most important bonders in a sacramental marriage are faith and values. When a couple shares a common, living faith and strives to live according to the same ethical values, they develop a deep bond between them. They must also use their communication skills to integrate their faith and values into everyday life. When they can do this, their sexual lovemaking will deepen their relationship. They will experience themselves as part of a "we" because of the bond between them and because of the bond they have with God. "From a valid marriage arises *a bond* between the spouses which by its very nature is perpetual and exclusive; furthermore, in a Christian marriage the spouses are strengthened and, as it were, consecrated for the duties and the dignity of their state *by a special sacrament"* (Codex Iuris Canonici, can. 1134, cited in *Catechism of the Catholic Church*, 1638). The bond between a married Christian couple is the essence of the sacrament of matrimony.

 ## LISA

Consider how glue holds two things together, making them one yet retaining the substance of each. Many people are concerned about the need to change when they marry, or they want to change the other. But you can continue to develop your own interests and hobbies after you marry while making space in your heart and life for your spouse.

We married at Thanksgiving and Phil was anxious about getting my "permission" to go away for the Christmas bird count; didn't newly-wedded wives require husbands to be always at their sides! He couldn't believe he didn't have to bribe me or promise me anything. Just go and have fun, I told him. He was following his interests, it wasn't excessive, and I still felt connected to my new husband. I considered myself a very tolerant wife!

But a few years later when the children were small, Phil became over-involved in his work, going back evenings and weekends, often socializing with co-workers. Then I felt disconnected from him and sensed he was seeking escape from the commotion at home rather than just pursuing his interests. Had we known how to communicate using the skills presented earlier in this book, we could have bonded in a healthy way rather than struggle with each other and our circumstances. We resembled the "married singles" or "housemates" lifestyle: each of us came and left from the same home base, neglecting to give our best, our caring, and our vulnerability to each other.

Fortunately we persevered. The "glue" of our faith—in God and in each other—and our shared experiences kept us together until we made progress in communication. We started taking walks after dinner, letting the kids ride bikes or trikes ahead of us as we talked. (We found it less intimidating to hash out issues outside rather than in a closed space!) We became more courageous in letting each other know what was really going on inside of us. We made the effort to reflect on what changes we could make instead of blaming the other. Eventually when we went out together or were by ourselves for awhile, we enjoyed each other again.

PHIL

I feel great peace about the bond that exists in our marriage. This serenity has not come without struggle, however. Two things affect the way I experience our "we."

The first is my sense of personal freedom. I need to feel that I am free to be me and pursue my interests. Lisa has been very understanding; she also shares the same need. Nevertheless, sometimes my pursuit of outside interests has weakened our relationship, usually because it prevented us from spending time together. I felt distant from Lisa when this happened, and we tended to be superficial in our communication. This did not make me happy and I realized I needed to give more attention to our marriage. I now know I must go beyond "What do I want to do?" to "What does our relationship need?" The answer to this question gets me back on the right track.

The second element concerns taking for granted the bond between us. Sometimes my satisfaction with our relationship deteriorates into complacency and neglect. I notice this particularly when I feel an inner resistance to saying "I love you" or when I feel awkward asking for a hug. These two expressions of intimacy come easily for me when we are close. But when we have neglected the things that keep our relationship alive, the bond between us is weakened. Then it's time to get back to basics—communicating, praying for each other, and doing something fun together.

Thus even though the bond between us gives me peace, I am aware that it is not a static but rather a living bond requiring care and constant nurturing. *Doing* the things we are sharing in this book helps keep our relationship alive and growing. Simply *knowing* about them is not enough.

Dialogue Exercise

1. Describe the bond that exists at this time between you and your spouse. Think of a symbol that expresses this bond.

2. What kinds of bonders are most important in your relationship? How does each bonder join you together?

3. How do you experience personal freedom in your marriage? How does pursuing your own interests affect your relationship?

Chapter Fourteen
Sent Two by Two

*He summoned the Twelve and began to
send them out two by two and gave them
authority over unclean spirits.*

Mark 6:7

An old saying teaches that you can't give what you don't have, but you also can't keep what you don't share, especially in a sacramental marriage. Through the grace of the relationship a couple is better able to serve others. Couples frequently discover that serving others helps them grow as individuals, further enriching the marriage.

The ideals of service and marriage, however, must be balanced. When the relationship becomes too exclusive, there is too little service and love stagnates. On the other hand when there is too much service, the relationship suffers—even when the couple serves together. Lack of balance causes selfishness and burnout, and most couples experience these at some time. When we persist in the struggle to balance our couple needs with others' needs, we learn to avoid extremes, thus growing as a couple who can give and receive from each other and also share with others.

Service need not be restricted to the Church. As the Vatican II *Decree on the Apostolate of Lay People* emphasizes, service includes the arenas of work, play, and civic action. Wherever we go and whatever we do, we are called to give witness to our faith and values. A sacramental marriage helps us do this.

PHIL

The Scripture cited at the beginning of this chapter was read during the Engaged Encounter weekend Lisa and I attended shortly before our wedding. I knew I wanted to marry Lisa, but I also wanted to do something to help spread the Gospel. I felt these were conflicting desires. Discussing this Scripture passage later helped me resolve this conflict. Lisa and I were being sent by Christ as a pair, just as he had sent the apostles to preach the Good News. Our marriage would give us the strength and support to serve God in whatever ways he called us.

I have been fortunate to find employment in the Church working as a lay minister, providing a variety of services. This work is fulfilling, but the hours are frequently long, involving evenings and weekends. Too many hours and demands make me feel distant from Lisa and empty inside, a signal to me that we need to give our relationship more attention. When I neglect this signal—I have, sometimes—I eventually become less effective in my service to the Church; burnout becomes possible. Only when I put first things first—

God, marriage, family, work—do I restore balance to my life.

Keeping our marriage alive while serving others requires constant attention. I need to recognize that my first call to service is not "out there" in the parish or diocese but rather in my home. Serving Lisa and our children is the best training I have ever received for lay ministry.

 ## LISA

Once, in the midst of preparing school lesson plans, organizing a pizza party for our religious studies class, returning phone calls from work, and contacting people about a church survey meeting, I thought to myself, *If I just didn't have a husband and family, I could really get all this done!* That startled me! I had become so focused on all of my service projects that my first priorities seemed a burden. Consequently, I took time to reevaluate my activities and priorities.

Service to church and community has always been a part of my life, even during my childhood and teenage years. A happy extrovert, I enjoyed the attention and satisfaction I felt serving others. I considered service work more important than anything happening at home. During a recent visit with my parents and sisters, we recalled that I was always going to meetings, extracurricular activities, and service projects, leaving my side of the bedroom a wreck and ignoring my turn to do dishes. Tidy rooms and clean dishes were unimportant to me.

That thinking continued until the startling thought that my family interfered with all my projects. I then began a new journey; I began to view my service in our home in a new way, seeing how important my acts were to each family member. My new perspective resulted in feelings of satisfaction from my service within our home, though I still enjoyed doing a considerable amount of work for others outside the family. I know I'll never be a wife and mother whose life is solely family-focused, but if I can keep my husband and family my first priority, I know I will be happy. Phil and I have agreed that before I say "yes" to any project, class, or presentation, I will first discuss it with him. I'm not seeking permission but rather making space for my logical side (or his logic if I'm not yet in touch with mine!) to consider the time commitment, the values of the project, and the consequences to our family. I still do much outside the home, but the family begrudges my outside activities less because we've considered them together before I've made a commitment.

Dialogue Exercise

1. How does your marriage help or hinder your service to others?

2. How does your service help or hinder your marriage?

3. What kind of service do you feel called to share at this time?

4. What do you and your spouse need to do more or less of to balance the ideals of marriage and service?

Chapter Fifteen
Marriage Is a Vocation

Live in a manner worthy of the call you have received, with all humility and gentleness, with patience, bearing with one another through love.
Ephesians 4:1-2

How many times have you heard prayers of petition for increased vocations to the priesthood and religious life? It seems the word "vocation" is almost always used in reference to those special callings. This is unfortunate because we consequently fail to appreciate that marriage, too, is a vocation, the one to which most people are called.

Why is it important to know that marriage is a vocation?

A vocation is a calling by God to a particular state of life in which one works out one's salvation. Any state of life includes some inconvenience and suffering; knowing that marriage is a vocation helps us remain committed to our duties and obligations when we experience the cross in our lives. It is the cross that can open us more fully to relying on

God for our happiness. In marriage we experience the paschal mystery, dying and rising again and again, confronting our selfishness, yet persisting in the struggle to love. Only by carrying our crosses is our self-centeredness healed and our hearts prepared for heaven.

Knowing that marriage is a vocation can help us remain committed to the relationship when we are tempted to give up and leave. Vocation means that God has called us to this state of life, that marriage was not just our idea but also God's. Therefore we can depend on God to help us love each other.

PHIL

You have probably heard the saying, "The grass is always greener on the other side of the fence." I have experienced this many times in married life. In my work as a lay minister, I have been privileged to be on staffs with members of several religious communities. I have sometimes envied their lifestyle and regretted my choice of marriage and family. This was especially true when I saw community members leaving at the end of the day to go home for an evening of prayer and leisure; I was going home to a tired wife, needy young children, and a long list of chores to do before bedtime.

At other times, the grass has looked greener in the person of another woman. I have met other attractive women and have thought I would surely have been happier married to one of them than to Lisa. These thoughts happened most frequently when Lisa and I weren't very close.

I certainly empathize with couples who have decided they can no longer live together as husband and wife. Marriage and family life are very difficult at times. When my feelings of attraction for Lisa have waned and when the stresses of family life have turned my eyes to the "greener grass" elsewhere, I have relied on my conviction that marriage is a vocation to help me persevere. I believe that God wants me to stay, and I know that my happiness comes from doing God's will. I do not know how couples can stay together without this belief.

What I have learned through these struggles is that my resistance to embracing the obligations of marriage and family usually arise from my selfishness rather than from defects in Lisa or the children. Married life has forced me to confront this dark side of my nature. If I had run to the "other side of the fence," I would have taken my selfishness with me and perpetuated the same cycle again somewhere else. By living out my calling, however, my heart has softened, and I have found a deeper beauty in Lisa and our children.

LISA

A sponsor couple for the local marriage preparation program was telling us how much they enjoyed hearing the priest give the Stages of Marriage talk. Though it did not seem to "click" with some of the engaged couples, our friends related to the concept of progressing from "Romance" through other stages to "Disillusionment" and then to either "Misery" or "Acceptance." I recognized the process from my high school dating experience. Initially I perceived a boy to be "perfect," then a "nothing," and finally "normal." At this stage we could become friends.

When Phil and I first married, I was sure we would skip the disillusionment stage! A few years later, however, I was ironing Phil's shirt, wallowing in self-pity and loneliness, tears streaming down my face. Other men seemed more sensitive and appreciative than Phil. Faithfulness was definitely part of my idea of marriage and I didn't want to hurt Phil. I didn't think our marriage was hopeless—he just needed to change! While I waited for Phil to change, I warded off temptations by recalling the maxim "If he cheats with you, he'll cheat on you." This helped keep me realistic about someone else being my new prince charming. I hung in there with Phil, through thick-headedness (from both of us) and thin-skinnedness (taking offense at every remark). Finally, through spiritual direction, retreats, and reflective prayer, I began to see, bit by bit, my part in making the misery. God's love for me became more and more personal as I scrutinized issues, ideas, and personality characteristics. Phil underwent a similar process, though in a different way. Because of the personal spiritual work we did individually, we became more tolerant and accepting of each other.

Our children felt more secure at home too, something that should be an outgrowth of the marriage vocation. They had friends whose parents had divorced; when we were angry with each other our children worried that we would divorce too. Some couples I know stay together for the sake of the children. I think that if they aren't working on themselves emotionally and spiritually, they probably aren't doing their children any favors by staying together.

LiVING
TOGETHER

Dialogue Exercise

1. Marriage is a vocation. What does this mean to you?

2. Describe a time when you felt like running away from your marriage and family commitments. What helped you stay?

3. How has married life helped you become a better person? How have you seen your spouse become a better person?

Part Four: LIVING TOGETHER

Chapter Sixteen
Money Matters

No one can serve two masters.

Matthew 6:24

Matthew's quote is just one of many negative or cautionary references to money in the Bible. Jesus laments, "It will be hard for one who is rich to enter the kingdom of heaven" (Matthew 19:23) and Timothy considers the love of money to be "the root of all evils" (1 Timothy 6:10). Yet in our society, money is essential. The task of a Christian couple, then, is to use money without getting spiritually side-tracked or trapped. Some potentially troublesome areas include: working at a job that pays "good money" but either splits the family or brings no personal satisfaction; being persuaded by ever-present advertising that you need new products and conveniences; buying on credit when you are unable to pay the balance due each month; and consistently using shopping as recreation or entertainment. What is wrong with these? They promote a focus on acquiring things or the money to pay for things. Because our life-center can be on only one thing, we will lose our focus on God if our focus is on something else.

As Christian couples we must find ways to combat or counter the temptations. These can include: supporting each other in getting the education or training needed for satisfying work; arranging work schedules to give spouse and family enough time to satisfy relationship needs; saving money to pay in full for new purchases; turning off television and radio commercials; ignoring continually arriving catalogs and television shopping channels; praying about pending major financial commitments and considering how time and energy will be re-structured; and reflecting on how our financial lifestyle contributes to or inhibits our spiritual growth and marital intimacy.

 ## LISA

After Phil and I talked about finances during our Engaged Encounter weekend, I relaxed. I'd been told that financial issues accounted for a high percentage of divorces; since we had discussed finances, I anticipated no problems! Actually, for several years we did agree on what to do with the tiny bit of money we had. But then came the time I mentioned in an earlier chapter when I went shopping almost daily, seeking adult interaction. I focused on not missing sales, buying items we really didn't need. I wasted opportunities to spend quality time with my children as I dragged them around behind me. And I spent too much money on "junk." When Phil expressed his concern about my spending, I became defensive and chided him about trusting in God to provide what we needed. Eventually, I agreed to make a budget with him, which greatly relieved his anxiety. But because my overspending had become rooted in something other than a lack of organization and planning, I continued to find ways to ignore the budget and get what I wanted. I had discovered that doing what I wanted with the money gave me a feeling of power. Control and power had thus replaced boredom and loneliness. Gradually I changed my passive habits and helped my "inner child" grow healthier. As I began asserting myself in other areas of my life, I had a less desperate need to control the money. I could truly work with Phil on the budget plan we had drawn up which included some personal spending money for each of us.

PHIL

I have read many times that finances are a primary source of stress for married couples. In my counseling work I have seen many examples of this. One memorable case involved a couple who had a combined income of over $300 thousand per year. The wife had just become pregnant and she wanted to leave work for a few years to be home with their child. Her husband objected because he worried about how they would pay the bills without her annual $60 thousand contribution. Although I found it difficult to feel sorry for this couple, I knew this was a real source of frustration for them. It also helped me understand that financial stress is often unrelieved by additional income—especially when a family's spending habits correspondingly increase.

Happily, financial stress has not been a major factor in our marriage. Neither Lisa nor I have expensive hobbies and the things we enjoy most are inexpensive. Together we earn enough to pay the bills and save a little for future needs. If we had more money we'd probably spend it on things we don't really need, and I doubt we'd be much happier.

In addition to our simple lifestyle, I think another reason we've avoided financial stress is because we learned early about the importance of following a budget. Without a budget, I would have had no basis for confronting Lisa about her spending habits, nor she mine. When one of us has needed or wanted to spend more than the budgeted amount in a particular category, we have discussed it with the other. Our requests have not always been well-received by the other because more money spent in one area means less in another. We have had to use our negotiating skills to work through these conflicting needs. Our budget is a negotiated agreement that expresses our values and priorities.

I believe it is important for each partner to have some personal money to use as each decides. This does not necessarily require his and her bank accounts but rather something akin to a monthly allowance. As long as she does not overspend, I do not question Lisa about how she spends her personal allowance, and she respects my freedom in this area also. This helps alleviate many tensions that would arise if either of us had to always go to the other every time we wanted spending money.

Dialogue Worksheet

Responses for each of the statements below are:

A-Strongly Disagree   B-Disagree
C-Agree   D-Strongly Agree

In the space provided write the reason(s) for your evaluation.

_____ 1. I seldom worry about our ability to meet our basic financial obligations.

_____

_____ 2. I am satisfied with our present system of paying bills.

_____

_____ 3. I am satisfied with the amount of income my spouse contributes to our family.

_____

_____ 4. I believe my spouse is careful about spending money.

_____

_____ 5. My spouse seldom nags me about the way I spend money.

_____

_____ 6. I believe my spending habits require no change.

_____ 7. We discipline our spending according to targets set in our family budget.

_____ 8. I am satisfied with our current standard of living.

_____ 9. My spouse is satisfied with our current standard of living.

_____ 10. My spouse and I agree on long-term financial goals.

_____ 11. My spouse and I are usually able to talk about our financial issues without arguing.

_____ 12. I trust my spouse with our money.

_____ 13. There is nothing about my spouse's spending habits that I want changed.

_____ 14. I do not see financial issues as a problem in our marriage.

_____ 15. More money would not make any of us happier.

Chapter Seventeen
Marriage, with Children

Be sincere of heart and steadfast,
undisturbed in time of adversity.

Sirach 2:2

Watch a couple prepare a space and arrange baby items
as they await the arrival of a new child. The nesting instincts
we feel at such a time—the desire to provide for a child; the
readiness to care for a child; and the anticipation of sharing
life, wisdom, skills—are all part of what the church considers the "procreative" aspect of marriage. It is a holy time
when a couple opens their hearts and lives to a new child.

What a sadness if later the couple discovers they have
grown apart during the child-raising years. What a frustration and struggle when differences of opinion about discipline cause a couple to undermine each other's authority.
How can these be prevented? We must be aware that when
children enter our lives, our own unresolved childhood feelings and fears resurface. How our parents raised us may have
been less than perfect, but we will defend even harmful acts

unless we have dealt with the emotional experiences of our childhood. As we become aware of the past's influence upon our present, we must find a way to share this with our spouse and to listen to our spouse's sharing with a gentle heart. The communication skills presented earlier in this book will help you. In addition, another appropriate step is to read a parenting book or enroll in a parenting class. We recommend several in the Suggested Reading section.

When children's illnesses, handicaps, traumas, and school difficulties occur, they add additional challenges for a couple. Grief, fear, frustration, and worry can tempt you to blame each other. Avoid this. The past cannot be changed and "If only…" torments away all hope for peace of mind. Stop such thoughts and pray for God's will. No matter what happens, God is with you. In the midst of your struggle, let God love you and your child. Remember that God loves your child even more than you and desires that you lead your child in a holy way through all adversity.

Whatever your situation, whether newly married, married again with a blended family, or "old married folks" with many kids, it's never too soon or too late to insist on scheduled couple time for yourselves, even at home. Time together at home is cheaper than hiring a sitter, and the children will sense the unity between the two of you. They will learn that parents are still people after they marry.

 ## PHIL

It has been a joy for me to be with Lisa when our three children were born and to watch them grow toward adulthood. In many ways our children have helped us grow. Their needs challenged us to depths of giving we would have never discovered otherwise, and their love for play and fun has fostered the development of the child within each of us.

Children have challenged my relationship with Lisa, however, in two major areas. The first and most important has concerned priorities. At times I felt I was on the outer orbit of Lisa's world, circling around her involvements with the children, her work, and her hobbies. She didn't seem to have much time, energy, and creativity to bring to our relationship, and I felt lonely and disconnected. It seemed that she wanted me to be a coparent of our children and little more. This bothered me a great deal, and I made many negative comments about how she spent her time and energy at work and in volunteer projects. I had difficulty confronting her about her involvement with our children, however. After all, they did have many needs and I supported the things she was doing with them. But what about *us*, I wondered. When are we going to get back to being best friends and lovers? When our children move away from home? I didn't want to wait that long!

Every time I broached this subject with Lisa, she quickly agreed that her values had not changed; our marriage had to take priority over raising children without neglecting their needs. Our challenge was to find a way to assert and cultivate this priority amidst the many demands of parenting and working. Choosing to make our marriage a priority has meant we have had to occasionally do something without the children; even when home with them, we need to find time to talk and be Phil and Lisa rather than coparents.

Parenting skills have presented a second challenge to our relationship. From our counseling experience we knew it was important for us to be united in our expectations of our children and agree on the consequences we would allow them to experience for misbehavior. As in many other marriages, however, one of us was generally more permissive than the other, resulting in frustration for each of us and for our children. Having a common set of values has helped us resolve this problem, but our growth in parenting skills has also been beneficial. Lisa teaches courses on parenting and she has shared much with me about effective ways to influence children toward healthy behavior. Our weekly family meeting also provides an opportunity for our children to share their feelings of gratitude and frustration about living together in a family.

God first, marriage second, and children third: these continue to be both my and Lisa's priorities. Significant shifts in these priorities create difficulties. Maintaining these priorities is a choice we will have to continue making for many years.

LISA

Even before we were married, Phil and I had picked first and middle names for twelve children. I'd seen how playful Phil was with his nieces and nephews, and I knew from years of baby-sitting that I really liked children. Reality challenged our dreams, however. We weren't physically or emotionally prepared for sleep-deprivation, schedule negotiation, and constant sickness, plus all the other daily needs of children. We tended to blame the other for not helping enough, or one of us would feel like a martyr for going the extra mile. Life is so intense when there are little ones who need constant supervision and lots of attention. When Phil and I finally had an evening out we usually went to church community functions. We'd talk to others but not to each other. If we could live those years over, I know we'd take more time just for us. Now, we "close up shop" at the same time each night; we are in the house with an invisible "Do Not Disturb" sign. It's our time to sip herbal tea, sit in the rockers or get cozy on the couch, and just talk about the day, the future, our feelings, or anything else. Intimacy and affection come quite naturally when we have regular times to be real with each other. Phil's frequent hugs and kisses throughout the day have also made an impression on the children, in addition to making me feel special! One of our girls recently commented, "Boy, when I get married, I sure hope my husband and I get along like you and Dad." Since we have learned how to meet our needs and theirs, we get along much better. In addition, the challenge of leading them spiritually has sparked many interesting conversations between Phil and me and among us all as family.

Dialogue Exercise

1. God first, marriage second, and children third. Are these your priorities? Have you been living according to your priorities? Explain.

2. What are some ways that raising children has helped enrich your marriage?

3. How does raising children test your marriage?

4. What do you need to do to avoid the trap of becoming coparents rather than best friends and lovers?

Chapter Eighteen
Handling Stress

Have no anxiety at all, but in everything,
by prayer and petition, with thanksgiving,
make your requests known to God.

Philippians 4:6

The media constantly inform us about the ill effects of stress on our bodies: heart attacks, ulcers, and susceptibility to sickness increase. Additionally, the emotional symptoms of stress (for example, short tempers, headaches, and preoccupation) create an environment inconducive to love and sharing. But the media shares the good news too: we can reduce stress in our lives and cope more effectively with the unavoidable. Don't be fooled, however, into thinking that only bad things create stress. Popular stress inventories include among the greatest stressors such positive events as birth, marriage, job promotion, starting school, and graduation. Stress brings feelings that can settle in our bodies and pollute our minds if we permit it. Exercising and doing physical activities that release stress from the body's cells are effective strategies for managing stress. "Self-talk" is another; become aware of negative or defeatist thoughts and replace them repeatedly with positive ones, thus keeping the mind from dwelling on negative images, past embarrassments, and worry. Daily habits of exercise and meditative prayer help calm and cleanse us, refocusing our energy on God whom we can trust no matter what the stress.

LISA

A friend who is a principal has a poster in her office: Your failure to plan does not make an emergency for me. When I first saw it I experienced both admiration and panic! The motto succinctly reminds us of the societal implications of our responsibilities. But I also realized that if I procrastinated, I would be stuck! Much of the stress in my life has come from deadlines crunching in on me when I have procrastinated or engaged in the Extroverted Intuitive "let's think about it a while longer and see if anything else comes up." I've persuaded others to rescue me from my predicaments, often drafting Phil at the last minute to help. This was neither fair to him nor to our relationship. When Phil decided not to rescue me anymore, I still inflicted my stress on him; he had to suffer through my tenseness, frustration, and blaming others until I returned to "normal." As I faced the unpleasant consequences of my procrastination, I became more disciplined and improved the pacing of my projects.

Another source of stress has been a perfectionism through which I derived my self-esteem. Phil and the kids used to hate when we had company; during the hour prior to our guests' arrival, I was sharp-tongued, bossy, and unfairly critical of them in my determination to make the house perfect. A perfect house meant I was "good enough." I have done a lot of "self-talk" to get myself out of this trap of perfectionism. When I appear to be slipping into it again, Phil comments—kindly—on my mood, my preoccupation, or other symptoms. He neither judges nor gets sarcastic; he just observes. I then know I need to adjust my self-talk, take quiet time, or do whatever else is necessary to regain harmony and calm.

 ## PHIL

Years ago, when our children were small, I often came to the end of my workday and thought, *Now I go from the frying pan into the fire!* Though life has become less stressful for me at work and at home, the reality of stress still exists as does its potential to create problems for our marriage and for me individually.

The first lesson I had to learn about handling stress was to quit acting out. Stress makes me cranky and greatly diminishes my patience, making me more likely to be short with others and harsh with my words. This tendency was especially aggravated when I returned home after work to find Lisa was also stressed. I became angry at her for being impatient and unaffectionate with me, thus increasing her stress. I had to stop making things worse for both of us, and I did so by either taking quiet time on the way home from work or by requesting a few minutes to myself after returning home.

Another lesson has been to recognize my stress signs. When I begin to shake my leg or pull on my beard, I know my body is stressed. I am usually hungry, angry, lonely, or tired (H.A.L.T.) and I need to pause and take care of my needs. Taking a short walk, writing in my journal, or finding a few moments for prayer is very helpful. My body type is such that I usually become hungry before the next meal is served; a small snack helps me stay calm. On days when I can nap, I do so; I would do well in cultures that schedule a midday siesta. As our communication skills have matured, Lisa and I have been able to share more honestly and effectively with each other during stressful times. I need to use each of these strategies at some time or another.

My most important lesson has been to learn that stress comes more from my attitude than from the external world. When I try to get or avoid something so I can be happy, I always have the fear that I won't get what I want. These disordered desires and the consequent anxiety cause most of my stress (and everyone else's too). Unfortunately, they are frequently present in my relationship with Lisa. For example, I may become convinced that I need her to act a certain way—perhaps calm, happy, or affectionate—if I am to be content at home. I sometimes become anxious about her response to my expectations. Having expectations is good as long as I can hold them in a spirit of detachment. This is difficult but I am convinced it is a key to living a relatively stress-free life.

LiVING
TOGETHER

Dialogue Exercise

1. What are the main causes of stress in your life? Remember to consider your expectations of how things should be.

2. What are some unhealthy ways you act when you are stressed?

3. What are some of the unhealthy ways your spouse acts when he or she is stressed?

4. What do you need from your spouse when you are stressed? Use the assertive approach to request this. Negotiate for it if necessary.

Chapter Nineteen
Work and Play

*The seventh day . . . [God] rested
from all the work [God] had done.*

Genesis 2:3

Despite the quote above, it seems impossible that God needed to rest after the fun and creativity of bringing a world into existence! If only all jobs were like that! But, though our work week is shorter now than two or three generations ago, we still struggle to find time for rest and re-creation for ourselves and with our spouses. A recent news report indicated that employers declare they want workers to be less stressed and have time for their families, while employees believe that unless they work overtime (paid or unpaid), they will lose promotions and maybe even their jobs.

How then does a Christian couple balance the demands of a boss who wants to beat the competition with their desire for time to develop a meaningful and intimate relationship at home? The self-employed find the balancing act even more challenging. Complicating the issue is the pervading tendency for men in our society to associate personal identity and self-worth with their work. Occasionally this degenerates into work addiction. True self-worth comes from the realization that each person is a beloved child of God rather than from the work a person does. When self-worth is rooted in this foundation, work becomes an expression of the desire to serve God. There is an openness to God's will in the use of each one's gifts and talents. It becomes possible to leave some tasks undone for the sake of spending time to play with those you love most.

 ## PHIL

In 1985, I decided to leave a secure, salaried position to enter the challenging but risky world of self-employment. I had many reasons for seeking this change; one of the most important was the prospect of spending more time at home with Lisa and the children. After a few months, I was home much more than before but only physically. I had difficulty setting a quitting time for my day—never a problem in my former job. I found myself constantly thinking about work and I was quite anxious about finances. Gradually I stopped calling on old friends and quit pursuing recreational hobbies like golfing and fishing. Self-employment brought me less time for play and family involvement. I was miserable.

Lisa worked full time then, often bringing work home. In addition, the needs of our small children took much of her time and energy. Yet she could say as surely as I that her work needed to be done and the children's needs must be met. Furthermore, we both had families who expected us to visit or call regularly.

Working hard, caring for children, and visiting one's extended family are good. Our problem was our gradual cutting back on time for us to have fun together. An evening out together became a rarity because we told ourselves we had so little time. The time *was* available but we just didn't take it. We relied on faith and communication to keep us together, but a marriage relationship needs more. Relaxation and play are also important for deepening the marriage bond; most spouses first begin to know each other on dates—dates that often revolve around fun and play.

My work could still be time-consuming if I permitted it but I have chosen otherwise. I have resolved to earn as much money as I can during a forty hour workweek, doing the work I enjoy most when possible. I also try to never take any work home with me, even mentally. I never do today what can be put off until tomorrow, but I do today what must be done. When I work, I work, and when I stop, I stop. This helps me be more present to Lisa and the children during my hours at home. This resolve has also helped me find time for play and fun at home as well as an evening out with Lisa at least once a month. I realize this philosophy goes against our culture but I prefer it to those days when I was too enmeshed in work.

LISA

I currently have the perfect out-of-the-home job for me: part-time, full of opportunities for creativity, serving and nurturing young people. Because I enjoy it so much, it seems like play instead of work. Thus it is temptingly easy to continue the fun on home time! When I do that too much, however, I hear hurt and frustration in my family's voices. Then I feel unhappy because in my exuberance I lost sight of my priorities and hurt them. I repeat this pattern whenever I assume too many responsibilities and get involved in too many projects at the same time.

I have discovered a simple time-management tool. I estimate how much time I will need to accomplish a task. Because I have a natural tendency to underestimate and because I am aware of this tendency, I double my original estimate. My new time estimates are very accurate! Another effective strategy is to include my family activities on my "to do" list: spend time with Phil, play ball with Paul, shop with Ri and T. Listing these activities gives them importance, and I am certain to do each item—even the fun things.

Dialogue Exercise

1. How do you feel about the balance between your work and play at this time in your life?

2. How do you feel about the balance between work and play in your spouse's weekly schedule?

3. What kind of fun or play do you most enjoy doing with your spouse? Do you experience this as often as you wish?

4. What do you need to do to create the balance between work and play that is best for your marriage?

Chapter Twenty
Putting God First

Seek first the kingdom [of God]
and [God's] righteousness, and all
these things will be given you besides.

Matthew 6:33

Recently a friend described how a Marriage Encounter weekend had revitalized his marriage. "I learned how easy it is to let other things come between me and my wife," he said. "The question that puts everything in focus for me now is, what do I need to do for the good of our relationship? When I put it this way, I can almost always see what needs to be done and I am more willing to do it, even if it calls for sacrifice." He told how this approach helped him move beyond a mentality of shoulds and obligations associated with his marriage. Choosing to do what is good for the marriage emphasized responsibility to his heartfelt priorities.

This same approach can work in our relationship with God. What do we need to do to keep or make this the most important relationship in our lives? The answer to this question is different for everyone, depending on where each is in the process of spiritual growth. Some may need to get back to church every Sunday; others may need a Scripture study group or faith-in-action group. Still others must send the crowds away and go to their private rooms, away from children and telephones, taking time to talk and to listen to God, sharing what is deepest in their hearts, hearing and knowing God's love for them.

Sometimes a person reports that a spouse became jealous of a partner's prayer time. This can occur when the partners differ in how important each considers his or her faith. The complaint can also arise when prayer doesn't gradually result in healthier love. The closer we draw to the Source of all love, however, the more love we have to share with the other.

There are many ways for you to put God first and to help your spouse do the same. As our friend suggested, however, you must ask the correct question: "What do I need to do for the good of my relationship with God?" Your honest response will also be best for your marriage.

 ## LISA

Once when I was seeking inspiration through spiritual reading, I came across a startling idea. A busy minister wrote that he spent an hour each morning praying with Scripture or in quiet reflection. When he faced a full schedule, rather than cut back or skip his quiet time, he spent two hours in prayer and meditation. I was shocked! That was contrary to how I planned my prayer time then. I had an "intuitive" approach: I prayed when I felt like it or when the Spirit moved me. Part of the minister's job was to pray and to talk to people about God. How could I be expected to do the same? When I tried to pray for an hour I failed—I got bored! I tried different kinds of prayer to fill the hour but that didn't help. To make matters worse, my husband's one hour in the morning wasn't enough for him. I wanted to put God first and I was jealous of Phil for being able to pray so easily. He never put me down but when he noticed my crankiness, he'd ask if I'd taken quiet time that morning. Many times, I had not.

Eventually, through spiritual direction and God's grace, I discovered that praying with Scripture each morning, even for fifteen or twenty minutes, really worked for me. "Worked" means that I felt God's care, love, presence, re-assurance, and even gentle chastisement couched in love. "Worked" means that I realized Jesus wanted to walk each moment of my life with me as my friend, brother, savior. No matter what our personality style, no matter what our background, that is the message that comes from prayer. I also realized Phil reached the same conclusions but from a different route. We could share; I didn't have to compete. That gave me great freedom. We still have different prayer styles today, but the proof of effectiveness is in the living and we are both aware of our own and the other's growth. During the day we both pause to refresh ourselves in God's love: he takes quiet time, I sing along with Christian music tapes. I treasure Phil's acceptance of me and of my style of spiritual journey—a few weeks ago he surprised me with a new tape.

PHIL

For me, the most important way to put God first is to take time for personal prayer. Communal prayer, like the Sunday liturgy, is good but it is not enough. I could never grow in my relationship with Lisa if I only communicated with her on Sundays in a large group of people. Just as I must take time to share with Lisa every day, so must I also take time to talk with and listen to God on a daily basis.

Without prayer I cannot keep God first in my life. When I "cut corners" on prayer, other things become inappropriately important—including our marriage. I begin to look for a depth of love and acceptance from Lisa that she is incapable of giving me. I also begin to use work as a means to validate my existence instead of a way to share my giftedness in gratitude. Without God as my center, the world rushes in and I become anxious and preoccupied. It is nearly impossible to love when I'm in such brokenness. I see the same consequences in Lisa when she neglects prayer.

Just as two lovers need to get away for an evening or weekend at times, so, too, do we need an occasional evening or weekend of prayer and renewal. We have taken turns going on weeklong retreats. Staying home with the children while Lisa is growing in the Lord gives me a deep sense of satisfaction. Also, when the children were small, we found it impossible to prayerfully attend Sunday Mass with them. Again, we took turns caring for them so that the other could grow in relationship with God.

Love of God and spouse is not an either/or experience for me. The surrender in love to God opens me to a deeper vulnerability to Lisa and vice versa. The more I love Lisa, the closer I come to God; the more I love God, the closer I come to Lisa. I know that it is God's will that I love Lisa, but I know, too, that I can never love her as much as God does.

Dialogue Exercise

1. What do you need to do at this time in your life for the good of your relationship with God?

2. How does your relationship with God enrich your marriage?

3. What happens to you when you lose the priority of God first?

4. How do you feel about your spouse growing closer to God? Are you willing to support him or her in this?

LiVING
TOGETHER

APPENDIX ONE
Descriptions of the Types

The descriptions of the eight basic types which follow are paraphrased from *Introduction to Type* by Isabel Briggs Myers. Use these descriptions to further confirm for yourself the insights about your psychological type to which you have already come.

A. **Extroverted Thinkers:** Use thinking to control environment or "run the world." Organize facts and opinions, define objectives, construct plans. Make good executives. Little patience with confusion, halfway measures. Can be tough and impersonal.

Shadow Side: Introverted Feeling. If neglected or not integrated, they can explode in damaging ways. Need to consciously make the effort to pay attention to their own and others' feelings.

B. **Introverted Thinkers:** Use thinking to analyze world, not run it. Love to organize ideas and facts. Focus their thinking on principles, underlying ideas. Detached, quiet, reserved, and logical until their ruling principles are violated. Sometimes have difficulty expressing ideas.

Shadow Side: Extroverted Feeling. If neglected, they are not likely to notice or take into account the feelings of others. Need to make conscious effort to affirm others and to avoid expressing disagreement over petty matters.

C. **Extroverted Feelers**: Radiate warmth, friendship. Make judgments based on personal, subjective values. Value harmonious relationships. Very sensitive to others' feelings. Enjoy people, visiting, talking. Conscientious and loyal.

Shadow Side: Introverted Thinking. If neglected, they get carried away with their feelings and may make decisions without properly testing facts and consequences. Without positive, inner self-talk, they are the most vulnerable to criticism and disapproval.

D. **Introverted Feelers**: Warm and enthusiastic but not outwardly so. Deepest feelings are rarely expressed. Governed by loyalties and ideals. Tenderness and passion masked by quiet reserve. They choose values independently; not influenced by others' judgments. They know what is important to them and protect it.

Shadow Side: Extroverted Thinking. If neglected, they become too idealistic and unreasonable, demanding perfection of themselves and others. Need to subject strongly felt convictions to practical feedback from others.

E. **Extroverted Sensers**: Adaptable realists. Notice facts and details better than any other type. Value and enjoy material goods, art, clothing, music. Unprejudiced, open-minded, fun-loving, patient. Enjoy the present moment.

Shadow Side: Introverted Intuition. If neglected, they become materialistic and superficial. Need to be open to the world of inner possibilities and energies.

F. **Introverted Sensers**: Sensation feeds their inner life. Ideas based on an accumulation of deep, stored impressions. Prefer things factual, accurate, not too complex. Outwardly calm, have a good sense of humor. The most thorough, painstaking, systematic, hardworking, detail-oriented type. Their perseverance stabilizes a group. Hard to stop once they begin something.

Shadow Side: Extroverted Intuition. If neglected, they become overly rigid and detail-oriented. Need to be open to new ways of doing things and willing to change course once a better way is indicated.

G. **Extroverted Intuiters**: Enthusiastic innovators. Always see new possibilities, new ways of doing things. Go all out in things that interest them and are interested in so many things they tend to complete none of them. Good motivators. Non-conformist. Highly independent. Adapt to people for sake of projects.

Shadow Side: Introverted Sensation. If neglected, they never stick to a task long enough to complete it. Become sidetracked, distracted by new possibilities suggested by stimuli from the outside world. Need to develop the discipline of following a practical plan to complete projects, continuing to work even when projects become boring.

H. **Introverted Intuiters**: Great innovators in field of ideas. Trust own insights more than authoritative or established claims. Great potential for single-minded concentration. Want to see their ideas worked out in theory and practice. Visionaries.

Shadow Side: Extroverted Sensation. If neglected, they are unaware of outside world or other people. Their focus on the future and with inner meditation may cause them to miss the present moment. Need the discipline of attending to details and sensory experiences.

APPENDIX TWO
Budget Work Sheet

If you do not yet have a family budget, use the work sheet below to help you prepare one. Keep track of weekly income and expenses in a record book or computer program.

INCOME	Yearly	Monthly
Salary: His	_____	_____
Salary: Hers	_____	_____
Interest	_____	_____
Other Income over $500 per year:		
Specific items	_____	_____
Miscellaneous Income	_____	_____
Total Income	_____	_____

EXPENSES		
Allowances: Hers	_____	_____
Allowances: His	_____	_____
Allowances: Children	_____	_____
Auto: Loan Payment	_____	_____
Auto:Fuel	_____	_____
Auto: Upkeep/Repairs	_____	_____
Auto: Registration	_____	_____
Bank Charges/Card Fees	_____	_____
Charitable Donations	_____	_____
Childcare	_____	_____
Clothing: Hers	_____	_____
Clothing: His	_____	_____
Clothing: Children	_____	_____
Continuing Education	_____	_____
Entertainment	_____	_____
Furnishings: Home	_____	_____
Garbage Pickup Fees	_____	_____

INCOME	Yearly	Monthly
Gifts: Christmas	_____	_____
Gifts: Other	_____	_____
Groceries/Household Items	_____	_____
Home Repair/Maintenance	_____	_____
Insurance: Auto	_____	_____
Insurance: Health	_____	_____
Insurance: Home/Property	_____	_____
Insurance: Life	_____	_____
Lawn/Yard	_____	_____
Medical: Dental	_____	_____
Medical: Illness	_____	_____
Medical: Wellness (vitamins, health club)	_____	_____
Miscellaneous Expenses	_____	_____
Mortgage	_____	_____
Postage	_____	_____
Professional Dues	_____	_____
Retirement: IRA/Keogh/Annuity	_____	_____
Savings: College for Children	_____	_____
Savings: General	_____	_____
School Expenses/Tuition	_____	_____
Subscriptions	_____	_____
Taxes: IRS Payment	_____	_____
Taxes: Real Estate/Personal Property	_____	_____
Taxes: State Payment	_____	_____
Telephone	_____	_____
Utilities: Electric	_____	_____
Utilities: Gas/Coal/Oil	_____	_____
Utilities: Water	_____	_____
Vacation	_____	_____
Other: expenses not listed that total over $500 per year	_____	_____
Total Expenses	_____	_____

SUGGESTED READING

Arraj, Tyra, and James Arraj. *Tracking the Elusive Human, Vol.1: A Practical Guide to C.G. Jung's Psychological Types, W.H. Sheldon's Body and Temperament Types, and Their Integration.* Chiloquin, OR: Inner Growth Book. 1988.

Bellecci-st.romain, Lisa M. *Building Family Faith*, Cycle B. Liguori, MO: Liguori Publications. 1993. Also *Cycle C*, 1993 and *Cycle A*, 1993.

Faber, Adele, and Elaine Mazlish. *Siblings Without Rivalry: How To Help Your Children Live Together So You Can Live Too.* New York: Avon Books. 1988.

Greteman, James. *Creating a Marriage.* Mahwah, N: Paulist Press. 1993.

Kiersey, David and Marilyn Bates. *Please Understand Me: Character and Personality Types.* Del Mar, CA: Prometheus Nemesis Book Company, Inc. 1978.

Popkin, Michael A. *Active Parenting Today—Parent's Guide: For Parents of 2-12 Year Olds.* Marietta, GA: Active Parenting Publishers. 1992.

Powell, John, S.J. *The Secret of Staying in Love: Loving Relationships Through Communication.* Revised edition. Allen, TX: Tabor Publishing. 1990.

St. Romain, Philip. *Lessons in Loving: Developing Relationship Skills.* Liguori, MO: Liguori Publications. 1989.

Whitehead, Evelyn E., and James D. *Marrying Well: Stages on the Journey of Christian Marriage.* New York: Doubleday. 1983.

OTHER LIGUORI/TRIUMPH BOOKS
ON MARRIED LIVING:

Gallagher, Chuck, and Mary A. Seitz. *Good News for Married Lovers: A Scriptural Path to Marriage Renewal.* Liguori, MO: Liguori Publications. Reprinted 1992.

Rabior, William, and Jack Leipert. *Marriage Makers, Marriage Breakers: Counseling for a Stronger Relationship.* Liguori, MO: Liguori Publications. 1992.